Selah

Liv Dooley

TBKS Christian Resources
Las Vegas, Nevada

Selah/ Liv Dooley —3rd ed.
ISBN 978-1-0881247-8-9

LIV DOOLEY

There is nothing Liv Dooley loves to talk about more than the Word of God. She is a Bible teacher and the podcast host of The Best Kept Secret with Liv Dooley, which has featured some of the leading teachers and burgeoning ministry leaders of our day.

Liv is passionate about helping people enjoy greater intimacy and authority in Christ Jesus through prayer. She is featured as a contri- butor with She Reads Truth and the YouVersion Bible app, and you can also find her writing on a variety of other apps, as well.

When Liv's not writing or podcasting, you can find Liv hiking a mountain, taking a road trip with her husband, or curled up in the corner with a good book. You can connect with her at livdooley.com or follow her on Instagram @candidliv to connect with her.

DEDICATION

To the mentors who taught me what it looks like to worship the Lord freely. I could never thank you enough.

TABLE OF CONTENTS

Introduction.. 1

Part One: 1 Samuel.. 7

Session One: Worship Invites You to Remember........................... 9

Session Two: Worship Invites Repentance................................... 33

Session Three: Worship Invites God to War 61

Part Two: 2 Samuel.. 83

Session Four: Worship Invites Renewal.. 85

Session Five: Worship Invites Resilience in the Wilderness........... 109

Session Six: Worship Invites You to Rejoice................................. 135

Appendix A.. 163

Endnotes... 166

Acknowledgements.. 170

INTRODUCTION

Hey Y'all

I am not what most people would call a worship leader. Never have been. Never will be. The only place I can hold a tune anyone would want to hear is in the dead center of a church with an incredibly gifted, and might I add *loud*, worship team. However, we know better than to confine the term "worship leader" to one person calling out to God through the lyrics they sing from the altar in front of a crowd of people. A worship leader is so much more.

While I may not be a worship leader in the cultural sense of the word, I am a woman who loves God. Why? Because despite the rejection I've experienced, He's never rejected me. Despite the rebellious years I spent running, He's done nothing but woo me to Him. And even though I have experienced deep regret, He loves me anyway. I have struggled with intense remorse over mistakes I've made in my past, and if I'm going to be truthful, mistakes I continue to make right on into this present moment. Yet the one thing that has helped me through all of it is the spiritual practice of worship.

Worship is not an instant remedy you can just engage to start living a life you enjoy. After all, it's not about us. More importantly, though, it helps us mark a lifestyle shift. It's true that the feelings of rejection waned in His presence, and my rebellion was healed at the root. Even so, I have found that regret waited. It waited until my breathing had returned to its regular beat, and I had begun to believe again. Regret waited until I had finished declaring the Word over my broken will and reveled in the wonder our Incredible God alone produces. It waited, and for a moment, it felt as if regret had won because there was a shift I still needed to make.

At one point or another, we will all experience rejection, rebellion, or regret, and many of us will experience all three. Still, what never fails to surprise me is how persistent regret is and how it waits on us to finish the physical practice of worship. You know, the part where we lift our hands and trust our Healer for the wholeness He alone can provide.

It is my prayer that this study will help you learn to foster greater faithfulness in the presence of the Lord despite any negative emotions that persist in your life. Regret is resilient because it continues to redirect our attention back to our shame and our sorrow. However, regret does not have the final say, and neither do rejection nor rebellion.

I have discovered that choosing to pause redirects our hell-bent hearts back to worship. Choosing to pause helps us pray and pay attention to God's direction with greater clarity than before. Choosing to pause reminds us that God is bigger than any of it, and that pause is scriptural, too.

Selah is a symbol that is included throughout many different Psalms, starting with Psalm 3, which was written by King David. It is also found throughout a prayer in the third chapter of Habbakuk. Although there is no modern-day translation, most believe that the symbol denotes an opportunity to pause based on where it is placed at the end of various verses.[1]

The symbol is so obscure that it could even serve as a synonym for the Hebrew word *forever.*[2] However, whether it is a liturgical tradition or a literary term, the placement of it continues to draw our attention to God as we contemplate its meaning and God's mercy.

Selah represents the delightfully glorious mystery worship encompasses in every way. It reminds us how important it is to pause when negative emotions persist. Selah helps us slow down long enough to reflect on God's goodness regardless of whether we feel good or not, and it offers a way to respond with wisdom in our reactive world.

The New American Standard Hebrew Lexicon defines the Hebrew word selah (סֶלָה) as to lift up or exalt.[3] As we surrender to the pause, we settle down to worship, sensitive to the many ways we exalt God's name above our emotions. Worship renews our minds and helps us reengage with the Lord in new ways. It reminds us He is worthy in everything, despite everything, and because of everything, a message King David expounded upon many different times.

King David, the man who rose to power throughout First and Second Samuel, wrote seventy-three of the 150 psalms.[4] He was well acquainted with what it meant to selah, and his choice to pause, worship, and pray to the Lord in the middle of rebellion and regret saved his ministry and his reign. King David teaches us an important fact I pray we never forget: there are no depths of despair that we cannot worship our way out of. The Lord is always ready to save us when we acknowledge His sovereignty in the middle of our rebellion and our regret when we repent.

Family, I believe that you are in the middle of a significant transition, much like the Body of Christ as a whole. It's my prayer that, together, we can ask God to heal us of any lingering rejection, rebellion, or regret that has attempted to hide in our hearts. In turn, I believe that when we do, the Lord will renew our will to wait on His perfect timing and help us develop the resilience the approaching days demand. However, should we resist the invitation to selah and continue to strive after our own impulses and aspirations, it is possible that we may suffer from even greater consequences. After all, many people included in the books of 1 and 2 Samuel are also willing to testify of that.

As we journey through 1 and 2 Samuel, we will find that when we trust God with our transitions, we can always look back and trace His faithfulness through the tests and temptations we faced. Worship will renew your mind and reveal God's glory. It will redirect your attention to the great things He's yet doing every time. It will draw your attention up.

Worshiping the Lord has taught me how to wait on His will, and it will always serve as my last answer to life's biggest questions. It's time to Selah.

HOW TO USE THIS STUDY

The books of First and Second Samuel are critical to understand because they share so much symbolism about the Coming Prophet, King, and Priest in Jesus Christ. Early on, you will see that there is a difference between Eli and Samuel, Saul and David, Michal and Jonathan, and many others whom we will study. That difference is revealed through their choices to worship or reject the One, True God as Lord. Lead with worship, and it will lead you to experience greater intimacy with the Lord. Leave it out of your decisions, and you will find that it has just as much power to isolate you from the Lord, too.

First and Second Samuel were originally composed as one book and were divided into two by the Septuagint (LXX), so we will take three sessions to explore First Samuel and three sessions to explore Second Samuel.[5] Although the writer, whom I will refer to as the biographer, is unknown, Jewish tradition ascribes authorship to the prophets Samuel, Nathan, and Gad.[6]

During our study, we will discuss themes such as the honor-shame culture and the collective nature of Israel at the time, and I hope you resist the temptation to overlook them. Today, we live in an innocence-guilt culture that is highly individualistic in North America. However, when we choose to read the Bible through the lens in which it was originally written, our revelation of the Word is enriched in every way.

This study has been created for you to enjoy both independently or with a group. It is your choice. Regardless of if you are enjoying this study with a few friends or you're exploring it in your personal time, I am here with you every step of the way to help you revisit old stories with fresh revelation.

We will be conducting an inductive study together, and you will find sample questions to work through during each study session. Still, I encourage you to dig even deeper beyond that. One of the biggest reasons God has used this study to speak into *my* life is because of the questions I asked of old Bible stories I'd long since heard and read. This is simply your starting place. God wants to meet us with fresh revelation every time we open His Word, so let's expect it.

I have created a mnemonic device using the word "worship" so you can remember what to do:

Watch the video teaching
Organize Your Thoughts
Read and Interpret the Text Each Day
Surrender The Areas of Concern that Rise Up
Humble Yourself to Hear What the Lord May Say to Your Heart
Identify Ways to Act on What You've Learned
Pray for the Lord's Guidance and Protection

Let's break that down more:

Watch: Every session begins with a video lesson that you can access through the QR code at the bottom of the first page for the first session.

Organize: Think about what we will be reading together throughout the week and establish what you already know about those stories.

Read: Read the passage each day and interpret the text by:
- Sharing questions that came to mind while reading the text and
- Investigating other scriptures that are listed, which you can cross-reference throughout this book, to benefit from a more comprehensive study.

Surrender: If you find yourself struggling to accept something we've covered, surrender it to the Lord by journaling about what felt hard to accept and why that might be. Ask God to take it from you, to loosen your grip, and to calm the worry that doing so might trigger.

Humble: This Bible study is written to help you grow more intimate with God, but our relationship is not one-sided. Prepare to spend time silencing everything around you so that you can hear how He wants to lead you to throughout the day based upon what we've covered.

Identify: The Bible is living and active, and these stories can teach us a lot about how to engage with our families and friends. Make a plan of action after every study to implement one thing we've reviewed.

Pray: Speak to God however you feel comfortable about what you loved in that session, what you learned, what confused (or still confuses you), what you're looking forward to, what you'd like Him to do, and end with praise for Him.

.

Praying for you,

Liv

PART ONE

First Samuel

SESSION ONE

Worship Invites You to Remember

Watch the video teaching
Organize Your Thoughts
Read and Interpret the Text Each Day
Surrender The Areas of Concern that Rise Up
Humble Yourself to Hear What the Lord May Say to Your Heart
Identify Ways to Act on What You've Learned
Pray for the Lord's Guidance and Protection

Watch the Video Teaching By Accessing It Through This QR Code

Organize Your Thoughts

SESSION ONE

Lesson 1

1 Samuel 1:1-3

Have you ever suffered from jetlag? What about jetlag that mutated into an incurable form of insomnia that lasted for weeks? Incurable is probably a stretch, as I have a tendency to exaggerate. Nonetheless, it was still brutal, especially since it felt incurable at the time. If you add a little negative thinking to the mix, you have a concoction for destruction- or at the very least, depression.

I will never forget the year I learned about the RAS, the reticular activating system, located in our brain stem. I had traveled back to the United States alone after visiting my husband in Korea, and I was miserable. My friendships were in a state of array, and I felt alone and isolated.

I spiraled into a series of negative thoughts night after sleepless night, until I discovered a neuroscientist and her work on the RAS. If you have ever wondered why you start noticing every pearl-white Toyota Highlander on the road after you purchase one, you can thank your RAS. It helps you sift through the billions of data your senses take in every second and filter through the unnecessary ones all with the intention of keeping you alive.[1]

In short, what you focus on magnifies. In 2016, I found it really hard to believe the Lord was doing anything good in my life. I was completely indifferent about the novel I was writing or the freedom I was enjoying in full-time ministry. Instead, I obsessed over all the things I wished I could change.

Once I realized that everything doesn't have to be good in order for me to acknowledge God's goodness, though, it changed everything.

Whether you have been caught running from all possible memories that inspire regret or you have been ruminating on them obsessively, worship is a gift you can access right here. Regardless of what has happened in your past, worship invites you to remember what the Lord has done.

Redirect your thoughts to all you have to be grateful for and who the Lord is in the middle of the loss you have experienced, and your RAS will

eventually follow. Since its primary job is to keep you alive, it will draw attention to that which is important to you.

Hannah chose to change her mindset about her challenges, and she is one woman who holds me accountable to this. We meet her in the first chapter of 1 Samuel, and I find it refreshing that the Lord decided to inspire such a significant series of events through a woman. However, she is not the only one the Lord was moving through at the time.

The book of Ruth took place during the time of the judges, which is also true of the first nine books of 1 Samuel. At the end of Ruth, we learn that Ruth became King David's great-grandmother when she gave birth to her son Obed.

We often overlook the transition from the book of Ruth to 1 Samuel, but it is likely that Ruth and Hannah walked through the streets of Israel during the same time in eternity.

Hannah, as we will learn, became the mother of Samuel, who served Israel into his old age before anointing Saul as the first king. Approximately twenty years into Saul's forty-year reign (Acts 13:21), Samuel also anointed King David.

Regardless of the exact time frame, both of these women are two generations removed from David. Furthermore, the book of Ruth compliments 1 Samuel to teach us what was going on in Israel's culture during the lifetimes of Naomi and Ruth when we first meet Hannah.

Israel, which had formerly been in a famine, was now thriving once again, and the crops were flourishing, which would have been reflected in their offerings to the Lord.

Unfortunately, the additional excess the Israelites now had to offer to the Lord exposed what was in the high priests' hearts. What does the Word tell us in 1 Samuel 2:12-17 about the religious culture?

Hannah carried the significant burden of infertility in a time and region where women were valued most by their ability to bear children. However, that wasn't her only problem. We see it through the introduction of a new name of God, as well. Jehovah Tsebaoth is translated as the Lord of Heaven's Armies or Lord of Hosts, and it first appears in 1 Samuel 1:3.

Why do you think it was important for Hannah to call on "Jehovah Tsebaoth"?

What could the author be communicating through the story, particularly as it relates to the use of God's name?

Define spiritual warfare (see video):

How did Hannah show integrity in the midst of spiritual warfare?

Hannah presented a beautiful balance of humility and confidence, intimacy and authority. What is the result of engaging in spiritual warfare when you rely on the Lord? (1 Samuel 1:17)

At the end of Chapter One, we see that Hannah was blessed with a son named Samuel, who wrote most of the two books we've come together to study. Once she had weaned the boy, Hannah took him to serve in the house of the Lord under Eli's mentorship, and the final verse states that he worshiped.

The biographers continue to talk about Hannah's influence on into chapter two, and it is here at the beginning of 1 Samuel that we see the stark contrast with which women are depicted in comparison to Judges. It is clear that God wants the Israelites to take note of how important women are in His plan for man's redemption. Redeeming them, and therefore Israel, from the abuse and manipulation the women were subjected to in Judges reinforced His plan to partner with women to accomplish something great on Earth.

In a prophetic prayer that resembles the Magnificat that Mary, the mother of Jesus, would sing in Luke 2, Hannah praised the Lord and prophesied about what was to come. Her prayer shows us the confidence God gives when we humble ourselves before Him. Furthermore, it demonstrates the boldness we receive to declare those things He reveals without fear of reprisal or retribution. Hannah was a long way from being criticized as a drunken woman, and the integrity with which she served the Lord proved that.

What stands out to you about Hannah's prayer?

What verses prophesy of what is to come? (1 Samuel 2:10)

As we will see, Hannah continued to serve as a prophetic voice and influence in Samuel's life, going so far as to make a mᵊ'îl for him, which was something only a high priest would have worn (1 Samuel 2:18-19). Still, the greatest sign of her strength and integrity was to entrust Samuel to the Lord and follow through on her promise, especially in such an evil society.

How would you describe Israel's culture as Samuel was growing up? Circle one:

Rebellious   **Ignorant**   **Attentive**   **Obedient**

Evil is everywhere, and even though it seems to be intensifying in recent years, we can take heart that it is nothing new, and neither are the solutions the Lord provides. He is and always has been faithful to save when we repent. Today, our culture has become obsessed with the law of attraction, psychic readings, and witchcraft because, like Eli and his sons, we have become overindulgent. Thankfully, the Lord can redeem us from anything-even from the grasp of hell itself, as we see in Jesus Christ.

Honoring God doesn't mean compromising our biblical values or adopting evil practices in a half-hearted attempt to show others how good our God is. Like Samuel, we can identify ways to elevate His name above everything that attempts to deny His sovereignty.

What purpose would the author have had in exposing the priests' rebellion? (1 Samuel 2:12-17, 22-25, 27-36, 3:11-14)

Through whom did God send messages to invite Eli and his sons to repentance?

When Samuel first heard the voice of the Lord, the Bible tells us he was sleeping in the temple, near the ark of the Lord (3:3). God speaks to those who spend time in His presence. We a so learn that His voice will not contradict His written Word. It convicts us, intending to bring direction or correction.

God spoke judgment against Eli and his sons. Yet, we do not read that Samuel worried about what was to come or what part he would play in any of it. Through Samuel's biography, we find it is crucial to wait and pray as we ready ourselves for greater responsibility.

How does 1 Samuel 3:19-21 describe Samuel?

When Samuel answered God's call, he consciously chose to elevate God's name above evil, and we have the same opportunity today. Integrity is an important component as we wait to see the Lord redeem His people from the evil in the, and it is one I hope we don't take lightly.

Integrity speaks powerfully about God's influence in our lives because it is born out of the intimacy we enjoy with Him. As God's influence grows in our lives, our influence grows in others' lives. When called to rebuke others, the message of correction originates in a place of love coupled with a desire to see people redeemed and restored to intimacy with the Lord, not canceled from fellowship in the Lord.

Let's consider others above ourselves as we ask the Lord to define and refine our character so we can stand against the tests that will undoubtedly come our way.

What do you believe about your call to serve the Lord? Have you focused more on the difficulty or the delight set before you?

Is there any compromise you need to repent of? Identify an accountability partner or ministry leader to confide in and continue to move forward with.

Worship leads you to resist worry and reminds you where your worth is found.

SESSION ONE
Lesson 2

1 Samuel 4-7

The Bible tells us all things work together for the good of those who love God and are called according to His purpose, and that includes the correction the Holy Spirit uses to communicate His great love for us (Romans 8:28).

God often uses areas of conflict in our lives to help us recognize our dependence on Him. Make no mistake about it: there is no evil in Him. He is not the author of confusion. He simply redeems the consequences to reintroduce us to the love He has for us.

Think of a time God disciplined you, and you found yourself feeling grateful for it months or years later.

When the Israelites went to war with the Philistines, they realized they no longer knew God the way they once had. They had drifted far from His plan. Spiritual warfare is the opposition we encounter from the enemy that challenges our intimacy and authority in Christ. The only way to defeat the enemy is through the Word of God in the presence of the Lord because that is where we learn to use the power of God's name.

What does Philippians 2: 10-12 say?

If we fail to spend time in God's presence, we forfeit every spiritual victory that belongs to us. After suffering a horrific defeat at Aphek, which killed four thousand Israelite men, the elders decided to bring the ark of God to the battlefield. What did the Israelites do when they saw the ark of God? (1 Sam 4:4)

Reflect on the ways we learn about God's omnipresence in Psalm 139:7–12 and God's manifest presence in 1 Samuel 3:10. Compare and contrast the ways they are similar and dissimilar.

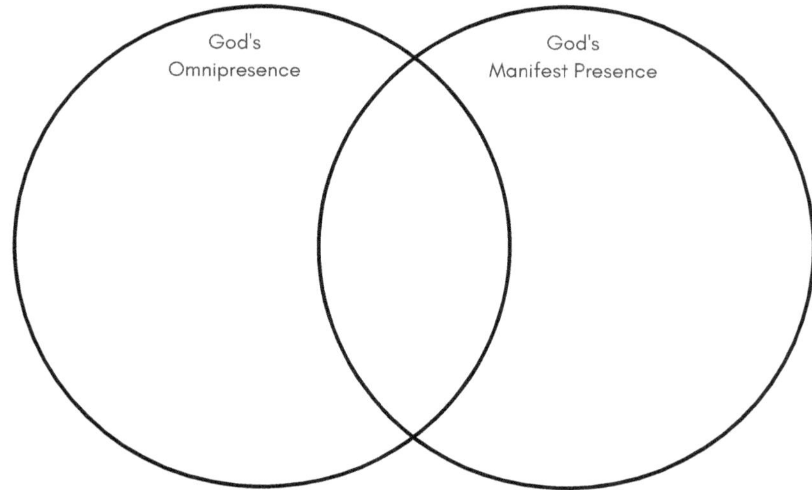

Unfortunately, the enemy knew what the people of God could do when God fought on their side, and it scared them. If only the Israelites had had a genuine fear of the Lord. They sacrificed relationship for empty religious practices and the supernatural presence of God for superstition. Their rebellion led them to sacrifice their intimacy and authority with the Lord, and as a result, the Lord allowed the Philistines to defeat them.

The Philistines killed Hophni and Phinehas and captured the ark of the covenant. Nonetheless, they didn't defeat or overpower the Lord of Hosts. They defeated Israel because her shouts had rung hollow when she called out to the Lord of Heaven's Armies in an attempt to manipulate His hand. Religion had failed them.

There is a difference between familiarity and intimacy. Familiarity is a byproduct of recognition, but intimacy is a byproduct of relationship. When we spend time with God, we move from simply recognizing who He is to finding safety in the authority we have in Him. With Him, we will do more than the enemy ever could. The Holy Spirit uses this passage to illuminate one important lesson: He never needs us. He just wants us.

What does John 4:24 say?

Are there any ways you have limited yourself by prioritizing familiarity (your knowledge of God and the proximity you enjoy with other Christians) above intimacy (developing a personal relationship with Jesus yourself)?

Why does the biographer tell us so much about the ark of God and the idol, Dagon in 1 Sam 5:1-5? What message is he conveying? Consider Philippians 2:9-11.

Find verses for those areas where you need to remember His sovereignty above your situation. Record them here.

The foreigners who did not serve God, although they feared and respected Him, hitched two cows to the cart carrying the ark. These cows had never been yoked and had no driver to direct them. However, the cows headed straight to Israel. They never got lost, and their journey demonstrated that God's plan always prevails with or without our help (1 Samuel 7:10-12).

When we realize God is all-powerful, we learn to worship Him simply because of who He is instead of what He does for us. The revelation of who God is also leads us to repent of our misconceptions and delight in Him anew.

How many years passed before the Israelites began to desire repentance (1 Sam 7:2)?

What did repentance require (1 Sam 7:3-4)

What did the Philistines do as Samuel was praying for the people (1 Sam 7:7)?

The Israelites place of prayer quickly became a battleground, but Samuel did not become distracted. He pressed into prayer and made a sacrifice to the Lord. What did the Lord do, in return (1 Sam 7:10-11)?

With Samuel's help, the Israelites learned to worship the Lord again. Their Ebenezer stone memorialized what the Lord had for them. From that point forward, it taught them how to elevate God's sovereignty above their situation.

Read 1 Samuel 7:12-14. What is the Lord inviting you to take note of and remember as He restores awe in your heart?

Access to Guided Prayer

SESSION ONE

Lesson 3

1 Samuel 8

Decades passed between Chapters 7 and 8 of 1 Samuel. In 1 Samuel 8, we learn that Samuel chose to appoint his sons as judges in his old age. Unfortunately, they didn't follow in his footsteps, and the Israelites began to make comparisons that led them to demand a king.

A comparison is, by definition, an examination of two or more items to establish similarities and dissimilarities.¹ In that sense, comparison is not a bad practice. We compare two banana bunches in a grocery store to decide which to buy based on our knowledge, preferences, and need. Many of us even develop a greater desire to learn the Word when we positively compare others' knowledge of and trust in God with our own.

I have seen God use comparison to move others (myself included) out of complacency. However, as with a lot in human nature, comparison can digress into guilt, shame, envy, conceit, and misunderstanding.

By Chapter 8, the Israelites decided to forfeit their freedom for the inferior confines of taxes and unjust, disobedient kings. Until that point, they had been led by God in a theocracy. However, they had decided they no longer wanted to be different from the other nations. Their comparison led to conformity.

Why might demanding a king deny God's dominion (1 Samuel 8:6-9)?

God had warned the people this day would come in Deuteronomy 17:14-20 as the omniscient (all-knowing) God. Aren't we all grateful we serve an omniscient God who knows everything and declares the end from the beginning? He had already prepared a solution, but first, He would allow the people to have their way.

What warning did Samuel give the people in verses 10-18?

What was the Israelites' primary motivation for rejecting God (1 Samuel 8:19)?

Review your schedule, patterns, and/or habits. What activities lead you to question God's goodness in the present moment more often? What comparisons are you most likely prone to make?

Activities that Lead Me to Question God's Goodness	Frequent Comparisons I Catch Myself Making

In what ways have you rejected God's plan for your life?

Celebrity culture (the obsessive adoration of famous figures)[2] now controls much of what we pay attention to and consume today. Saul's rise to power reveals that the concept itself is not all that new. In her book, *Celebrities for Jesus*, Katelyn Beaty explains that celebrities are manufactured to embody what the culture celebrates. The Israelites wanted, in many ways, a celebrity with whom they could align themselves to gain greater influence among the other nations.

Elevating others to places we should esteem God's presence alone always leads to pain. Thankfully, worship leads us to stop comparing ourselves with others and consistently humble ourselves as Christ always has. We have nothing to prove when the Great I AM is our defender.

How did the Israelites' desire for influence lead them to compromise their integrity (1 Samuel 8:19-22)?

Access to Guided Prayer

In what ways have you limited yourself and stifled the Holy Spirit by yielding to comparison?

What are our modern-day idols?

The Scripture That Resonated with Me Today

Thoughs that Come to Mind and Prayers From the Heart

SESSION ONE

Lesson 4

1 Samuel 9-11

Not *every* good opportunity is a godly one, and this lesson is painfully clear through Saul's ascent to the throne.

Upon meeting Israel's first king, he appeared to be the perfect candidate. The Bible tells us that Saul looked the part. Standing a head taller than everyone else, the biographer points out that Saul was the most handsome man in the land. Saul was someone a kingdom would naturally want to align itself with, and there was more. Saul seemed to be a loyal son and an honorable man.

What characteristics and actions in 1 Samuel 9:1-10 seem to demonstrate humility on Saul's part?

Saul seemed like the perfect choice. Yet, in spite of that, signs that Saul cared more about what others thought than what God says started to surface from the very beginning.

The people of Israel were spread across the land in tribes. When the Israelites who lived in Jabesh-Gilead were threatened by Nahash, the king of the Ammonites, they worried the other clans would ignore their pain.

What did the Israelites in Jabesh-Gilead agree to in 1 Samuel 11:2-4?

A quick study through a few chapters in Judges shows that the Israelites' doubt that their brothers would offer help was justified. They had long since experienced division from the other tribes because they had failed to hold the tribe of Benjamin accountable in Judges 19-21.

The tribe of Benjamin had committed heinous crimes against a concubine, and both the tribe of Benjamin and those living in Jabesh Gilead were punished for their complicity.

What tribe did Saul belong to (1 Samuel 9:1)?

What did Saul do to threaten the other tribes in 1 Samuel 11:7?

By doing this act, Saul evoked the specific imagery of what had been done to the Levite's concubine in Judges 19:29. In so doing, Saul associated himself with one of the most sinful eras and heinous acts in Israelite history.

God is a just God. He often uses challenges and conflicts to draw us into repentance, and sincere repentance is always accompanied by a commitment to obedience. God's justice flows from the marriage of His love and holiness[1]. Therefore, it does not diminish or replace the need for repentance or the pursuit of righteousnesss. When we refuse to acknowledge areas of compromise in order to avoid pain we underestimate the redemption God can provide.

How did Saul's actions demonstrate an alliance with rebellion over the redeeming nature of God?

Although Saul seemed to be the perfect king, those first few days revealed how much more important culture was to him than his connection to God. Saul's choice to align himself with an unrepentant clan without offering correction represented the tone of his tenure on the throne.

Consistent worship leads us to prioritize integrity over influence and to repent quickly when we recognize that we have confused the two. Where might you have prioritized influence over integrity?

How could Saul have helped Jabesh Gilead without hindering their growth (or his) in the Lord?

Access to Guided Prayer

Worship leads us to repent quickly.

Lesson 5

1 Samuel 12

Rejection is rarely about you. When others reject us because we're too loud, too quiet, too outspoken, too accepting, too demanding, too passive, etc., it is rarely about us. Rejection reflects the internal problems of the person projecting their insecurity on to others. Still, it feels nearly impossible to discern the difference at times, and the prophet Samuel struggled, too.

Who did the Lord state that the Israelites were rejecting (1 Samuel 8:7)?

Although it's not the last we will see of this mighty prophet who brought revival to a nation, 1 Samuel 12 serves as his last speech as the leader of the Israelites. As we continue to observe Samuel's life, we find that what he initially took for rejection was promotion. Though Samuel ceased to lead Israel, he began to serve as Israel's first advisor to the king.

During his farewell address, Samuel required the people to acknowledge how well he had served them. However, he didn't stop there. Samuel referenced an old lesson he had lived out his entire life and taught them in 1 Samuel 7:12. Worshiping the Lord reminds us what He has done for His people and for each of us in years past. Worshiping the Lord recognizes God's power to redeem anything.

What similarities do you see between Joshua 24:14 - 15 and 1 Samuel 12:14 - 15?

Corporate worship redirects others' attention back to God. It serves the dual purpose of honoring God and reminding others where to turn when no one else demonstrates reliability.

Samuel had been faithful, but his heart had broken to see them reject the Lord, so he asked the Lord to do one final thing to instill reverence in their hearts. What did Samuel ask the Lord to do? (1 Sam 12:17-18)

Understanding the attributes of God help us to worship Him in Spirit and in *Truth* (emphasis mine). God is omniscient, omnipresent, and omnipotent, but in order to appreciate these attributes, you must understand them.

Define omniscient (Look for a clue in Psalm 139:4):

Define omnipresence (Look for a clue in Psalm 139:7-12):

Define omnipotent (Look for a clue in Psalm 18:7-15):

How might praying for rain and thunder instill reverence in the Israelites' hearts?

Think of a time the Lord taught you how to reverence Him.

If anyone teaches us how to transition with integrity, it's Samuel. Continuing to serve, he reassured the Israelites that he would never stop praying for them. Worship leads to a powerful ministry of prayer.

May we all follow Samuel's example by resisting seeds of bitterness that attempt to seep within us after feeling rejection. Pray continually, without ceasing, even when it feels like your influence has been stripped away because integrity will stand in its wake (1 Thessalonians 5:16-18). It is there we evade the risk of regretting missed opportunities, and we see God's power of redemption on display. It is there we find an opportunity to partner with God and display humility. It is there God does some of His best work.

How has Jesus helped to redeem you from your past mistakes?

corporate worship redirects others' attention back to God.

SESSION TWO

Worship Invites You to Repentance

Watch the video teaching
Organize Your Thoughts
Read and Interpret the Text Each Day
Surrender The Areas of Concern that Rise Up
Humble Yourself to Hear What the Lord May Say to Your Heart
Identify Ways to Act on What You've Learned
Pray for the Lord's Guidance and Protection

Watch the Video Teaching By Accessing It Through This QR Code

Organize Your Thoughts

The Scripture That Resonated with Me Today

Thoughs that Come to Mind and Prayers From the Heart

SESSION TWO
Lesson 1

1 Samuel 13-14

Regret is a powerful emotion that evolves from the sadness we feel about mistakes we have made. It is a unique emotion because it is self-focused.[1] Consequently, it is easy to understand why someone might run from the opportunities to reflect on the past. It is also understandable how someone might get caught up reflecting on it too much. Thankfully, the Lord shows us He can redeem anything when we draw our attention upward. We just have to get honest about our part without unnecessarily holding onto it.

Regret often looms larger than life in our present mindset because of the perspective we retain about our past.

The key to moving forward in the freedom the Lord offers rests in our ability to recognize that our worth is not dictated by the wrongs we have committed.

Just because we have made mistakes does not mean we are mistakes. Take a moment to think about how God continues to lavish you with mercy.

What mistakes stick out from your past?	What have you believed about yourself as a result?	What does God's Word say about you?

The books of 1 and 2 Samuel bring us so much hope because it is through these narratives that we witness the many ways the Lord renews our minds when we choose the humility to admit we have been wrong.

As we have seen, integrity is built upon the intimacy we develop in the Lord's presence. It is that intimacy that will strengthen our faith in what the Lord is doing as we begin to recognize the difference between conviction and condemnation.

Conviction is the urge that rises within us due to Holy Spirit's leading. It serves as a tool to expose sin and establish us in the Word *before* we act in opposition to God's Word. On the other hand, condemnation is the feeling of guilt we are left with once we have made a mistake. It continues to remain with us as long as we allow the enemy to reinforce it.

What does Romans 8:1 say?

As we will see through our two central figures, Saul and David, fear of condemnation becomes a powerful tool the enemy uses to distance us from the Lord. In contrast, when we choose to grow more intimate with the Lord, we learn to respond to the conviction that rises to our hearts more readily. **The more time we spend in His presence, the more sensitive we become to His Spirit.**

Regret is a byproduct of condemnation, and it presents yet another reason we can be convinced it is not in the Lord's plan for our lives. Spending time in the Word of God helps us renew our minds after the Lord's as it begins to penetrate our hearts.

What does Matthew 12:34 say?

This week, we meet King David and are introduced to him as a man after God's own heart long before we learn his name. It is through his life that we learn spiritual warfare doesn't have the power to keep us from the Lord's promises when we continue to seek His presence.

Unfortunately, King Saul didn't recognize the power of God's presence. As someone who continually prioritized the people's approval above God's presence, he quickly began to elevate his own desires above God's directives, to his detriment.

When Saul and his men grew restless waiting for Samuel to come to

Gilgal, Saul's men began to scatter. Rather than encourage the men or rise up as their king to demand their alliance to the Lord, Saul oversaw the sacrifice himself.

Nothing can quench conviction and lead us to experience regret quite like striving outside of the Lord's presence. **Striving outside of the Lord's presence causes us to work to make things happen instead of waiting on God's timing.** It leads us to feel God serves us instead of the reverse.

Read Hebrews 4:9-11. What is the difference between striving in the Lord's presence and striving outside of the Lord's presence (Note the ESV)?

Appalled by what Saul had done, Samuel told him that he had forfeited further opportunities by ignoring the commands of the Lord and submitting to cultural pressures.

What does Samuel 13:13 say Saul forfeited through his disobedience?

What do you close yourself off to when you refrain from repentance? (2 Chronicles 7:14)

What does Joel 2: 13 tell us our response should be when we make mistakes?

In 1 Samuel 14:1-46, the biographer went to great lengths to describe Jonathan and a battle he fought. Why do you think the biographer was so detailed?

Prayer is communication with God, and it encompasses everything from the words we say to the facial expressions and body language we use. However, it's not unilateral or one-directional. It also involves the ability to listen and discern God's response through the written word He's revealed, the impressions or unction He places on our hearts, the rhema Word He speaks through others as confirmation, and the silence we sometimes meet.

Jonathan teaches us that when we pray, we don't have to be afraid of getting specific. He told the armor bearer exactly what he expected the Lord to do to reveal His will for them, and Jonathan trusted that the Lord would show him if it were not the right time for them as well (14:6). Do we?

Culture today uses words like "manifesting our destiny" and often promotes magic and witchcraft as a viable way to manipulate an outcome. As children of God, grafted in through the body of Christ, we invite the Lord to renew our minds about His will and what will benefit us.

When we choose to trust that God has the ability to bring about His glory and our good, we look to the Creator to discern the future and deny our petitions, even when it takes decades to discern how good that decision was. Manifestation and magic, by contrast, superimpose our will over His and lead us into rebellion. Remember, the fruit of the Spirit includes patience. Anything that leads us to force our will or manipulate our future is not of the Spirit.

What messages have you received from the culture about manifestation and magic?

Do those messages align with the Bible? Where do they differ?

The enemy invited Jonathan and his armor bearer over, reinforcing Jonathan's belief that this battle belonged to the Lord. As the war continued, the Lord fought on behalf of His people, but Saul's pride began to expose itself once again. What threat did Saul make in 1 Samuel 14:24?

What did Jonathan do in 1 Samuel 14:27?

Embarrassed that his son defiled his threat, Saul repeated his threat, this time personalizing it. Thankfully Jonathan lived with so much integrity, the people rose to Jonathan's defense, and Saul was further shamed.

What did the people of Israel say about Jonathan in 1 Samuel 14:45?

Jonathan couldn't have been more different than his father. Forgiving, gracious, kind, loving, humble, patient, gentle, and self-controlled, it was evident he had a heart for the Lord.

Which fruit of the Spirit do you struggle to cultivate most (reference Galatians 5:22-23)? Pray that the Holy Spirit would give you a greater desire to grow more disciplined in those areas.

What have you believed about yourself based on your parents' personal hangups and problems? What does Jonathan teach us through the way his character contrasts his father's character?

Identify a few scriptures to claim in those areas.

1.

2.

3.

The Scripture That Resonated with Me Today

Thoughs that Come to Mind and Prayers From the Heart

Lesson 2

1 Samuel 15

I hate butter pecan ice cream with a passion. It is perfectly good ice cream that someone decided to ruin with pecans. That is not my problem, though. I love ice cream. I can count on one hand the number of times I have declined the invitation to have some–even when it is butter pecan that is being offered.

When I was growing up, my Grandma Ruth's fridge was always full of ice cream. Unfortunately, one summer evening, the only thing that remained in her freezer was...you guessed it, butter pecan. I obligingly took some as the obedient granddaughter that I was, without ever mentioning my disdain for the flavor.

I commenced eating the ice cream over the sink, where I could expel the pecans as quickly as I consumed the delicious flavor surrounding them. Why I didn't consider the trash can was evidently too much for a seven-year-old brain to conceive. I can only imagine that I must have wanted to get caught.

Caught I was. To make matters worse, I, the only person in the house who did not enjoy eating butter pecan ice cream, insisted those mystery pecans in the sink had appeared out of nowhere.

My grandma knew it was me. My aunt knew it was me. I knew it was me. Yet I still withheld any semblance of guilt or an apology by pretending a secret bandit had broken in and left a few surprising pecans in the sink on their way out of the house. My grandma was less than impressed, but she waited me out. I finally decided that any punishment would be better than the torture I was subjecting myself to under her suspicious and unwavering gaze. I mean, 'Goodness! Wasn't she tired of looking at me?'

You can imagine my surprise when my little seven-year-old heart began to feel the comfort that accompanies confession. Sure, there would be consequences, and I would no longer be offered butter pecan ice cream (praise the Lord!). However, it all paled in comparison to the freedom that flowed from the renewed faith in my sweet grandmother's love for me.

Worship invites repentance, and repentance is anything but restricting. **Repentance offers freedom and a sense of finality in exchange for our ignorance and false indifference.** It offers the ability to remember you are not your mistakes as you strengthen your faith in the Faithful God's love that covers you through moments of crisis, no matter how large (or pecan-sized) they seem.

Saul struggled to balance calling and culture, and we continue to experience similar struggles today. However difficult it may feel to follow the Lord's commands when we think it restricts our loved ones, repentance helps us remember that our relationship with the Lord is founded on the reality that His love can reach beyond the impossible.

Humble leaders who submit to the Lord of lords and King of kings will always lead people to Life (John 14:6). Meanwhile, leaders who cave to cultural expectations close themselves off to the saving power of Christ. It's easy to forget that our God lives outside of the confines of time and cultural pressure. That's why it is important to humble ourselves at the feet of the One who sits high and looks low in order to grow in discipline when we lack insight.

What have you found yourself struggling to accept about Christ that contradicts cultural expectations and customs?

Cultural Expectations I Was Raised to Confrom To	Christ's Expectations that Contradict the Culture and Community I Love

Nothing ever surprises God. The Word tells us that Christ was known before the foundation of the world, so you can believe He knew the many ways the devil would be after the seed of the woman (1 Peter 1:19-20). During one of those instances, Satan even moved on Haman, the Agagite, to strategize how to kill Jewish people long after Saul reigned (Esther 3).

God knew it, so He set a plan to end the animosity between His children and the Amalekites (also known as the Agagites) once and for all. They first had strife when Amalek attacked the vulnerable Israelites while they were camping at Rephidim with Moses in Exodus 17. The Lord planned to save His children from further attack in 1 Samuel 15, but there was one problem: Saul cowered to the cultural expectations once again.

How do we know Saul was focused on himself? What did he do in 1 Samuel 15:12

A lot of us see the injustice of killing an entire people group as a reason to question God's goodness, but that was not Saul's motive by any means. The Israelites dishonored God by taking a profit for themselves when they exacted His judgment, ignoring the opportunity to reflect the remorse He feels when people fail to repent for their sins!

During Saul's day, it was customary for kings to enslave enemy kings to gain influence among other nations, and it is evident he only preserved Agag's life to elevate his pride. Unfortunately, Saul would have no problem killing the priests, but here he preserved an enemy king's life. Ironic.

This tells us two things: war was a part of daily life, and we all need Jesus.

When Samuel arrived, he chastised Saul and warned him that obedience was better than sacrifice and that listening should take priority above the most delicate offering. For rebellion is as the sin of witchcraft, and stubbornness is as iniquity and dolatry (15:23).

Samuel informed Saul that ritual performance was revolting, and it was the obedience that results from relationship that pleases the Lord. However, he didn't stop there. He instructed Saul that rebellion had the same spiritual root as witchcraft.

Witchcraft is practiced by people who attempt to manipulate their environment through mystical or spiritual means, and it defies God's will and rejects His sovereignty and personhood as the Great I Am in exchange for personal gain. Intentional or not, anyone who chooses witchcraft refuses to bow to Yahweh, demonstrating the work of the flesh, our sinful nature, through the choice to align oneself with Satan, the Father of Lies.

Samuel's accusation shows us that witchcraft can appear in the Church among some of the very people who lead our worship services. Matthew 7:15-20 tells us that we will recognize the children of God by their fruit. Here, Saul also shows us that we can discern what is influencing us by the motive or the priority that inspired us to act.

Modern-day forms of witchcraft include astrology signs, fortune-telling, tarot-card readings, psychic visits, manifesting, and white magic.

How have you been conditioned by the culture to view witchcraft and magic?

In light of God's Word, how do you see it now? Is it hard to accept the truth that all magic and witchcraft, including tarot readings and psychic fortune telling, stand in opposition to God's nature?

The good news is that the Bible tells us nothing can separate us from the love of God in Christ Jesus our Lord (Romans 8:39). Unlike the devil, who can never hope to be restored to God's favor and love, we always have the ability to renew our relationship with Him through repentance, which means to turn away, specifically, from our sin.

Pray this prayer with me if you want to be restored, too:
Father God, in the name of Jesus Christ, I bless You for the grace and mercy Yoi continue to extend over my life. Help me to believe in the ultimate authority, Your Word, despite what I have been conditioned and accustomed to believe in my culture. I repent of everything I have aligned myself with that is out of Your will for my life. Renew my mind so that I may learn to worship You in spirit and in truth, in Jesus' Holy name, Amen.

I am praising God with you! That is all it takes, and I truly wonder what would have been possible for Saul if he had turned once again to worship God as sovereign. Instead, he offered a half-hearted apology to convince Samuel to go with him to worship God in front of the people. Recognizing it as such, Samuel refused, and Saul grew violent.

What did Samuel tell Saul had been torn from him (1 Sam 15:28)?

Unmoved, Saul continued to demand that Samuel honor him before the elders, and his worship rang as hollow as they once had when Israel shouted before the ark of God in Samuel's young adulthood.

Unfortunately, Saul would turn more and more to rebellion, tempted by idolatry and witchcraft. He turned to a necromancer as his final resort, but that's a story for another day. For now, it is my prayer that we remember God is always ready to help us renew our minds and our relationship with Him when repentance is motivated by respect for His sovereignty.

Access to Guided Prayer

Thoughs that Come to Mind and Prayers From the Heart

SESSION TWO
Lesson 3

1 Samuel 16-17

In 1 Samuel 15, we read that the Lord said He regretted He had made Saul king. Part of the reason we sometimes struggle to connect with God is that we forget He has emotions. We were made in His likeness, and He gave us the ability to feel sadness, anger, pain, and disappointment. However, we often experience emotions that have been perverted and manipulated as a result of the fall, too. Take lust, for instance. As a perverted form of love, we often feel lust at the expense of pure, innocent admiration, and it infects the way we interact with God and others.

Still, we were never meant to live with regret, the deep sadness we feel as a result of a mistake we have made, and we see proof of this at the beginning of chapter sixteen. What word of renewal did the Lord send in 1 Samuel 16:1?

Unfortunately, a lot of us do the text an injustice by reading through the lens of our own cultural mores and customs. A cultural more is a norm or belief that cultures consider important and are accepted without question.[1] Because Western culture prides independence, individualism, and even secrecy, and we have the ability to ensure it is guarded, we often read the anointing of David as if it was a secret matter in the living room of an intimate family gathering. But it was not.

Why was Samuel afraid to go to anoint one of Jesse's sons (1 Sam 16:2)?

The anointing of David was not a private affair, as many of us are often led to believe. Who attended the sacrifice with Samuel (1 Sam 16:4-5)?

Before we go further, let's consider how excited the townspeople must have been and how many people would have known of it. The Lord used that opportunity to show that He uses foolish things to confuse the wise (1 Cor 1:27).

What does 1 Samuel 16:7 say the Lord looks on?

David's anointing exposed the depth of rejection David endured from his family. Even after Samuel passed over Jesse's eldest sons, once the oil refused to flow, Jesse still refused to volunteer that he had an seventh son. Why did Jesse finally send for his son, David (1 Sam 16:11)?

As soon as the prophet anointed the future king, we read that the Spirit of the Lord rushed upon David from that day forward, and it is here we learn just how different David was from Saul (1 Sam 16:13-14).

David would not be crowned kind of Judah for approximately fifteen years after his anointing, but God took him through a series of challenges to prepare him for his reign.[2] We notice him begin to grow in influence almost immediately after his anointing, which reveals that when you pursue intimacy with the Lord, He adds the increase.

What happened to Saul in 1 Samuel 16:14?

This in no way projects any limitations on the Holy Spirit. The Holy Spirit, the third part of the Trinity, has always been present. In fact, we meet the Holy Spirit first in Genesis 1:1. The Spirit is omnipresent (Ps 139:7-8) omniscient (Isaiah 40:13), and omnipotent (Zechariah 4:6).[3] However, it wasn't until Jesus rose from the grave and ascended to heaven again that Holy Spirit began to fill us and indwell in us as believers in Christ (John 6:7). Up until that point, the Holy Spirit rested upon people and filled them to fulfill important acts of obedience temporarily. As Christ's followers, we can grieve Him and quench His Spirit through sin and contempt, but we can't lose Him. That is the grace Jesus Christ brought into our lives, but it was one Saul couldn't access, and so he was turned over to the torment his rebellion had attrccted (Ephesians 4:30; 1 Thessalonians 5:22).

Why did David first go to the palace (1 Sam 16:16-21)?

Through David's service, we learn that worship changes the atmosphere and serves as both an offensive and a defensive attack against the Enemy. Worship helps renew our minds about the Great God whom we worship and contrasts worry, which leads us to rely on our own strength.

When recommending David, I find it interesting that they acknowledged him as someone who was skillful, brave, wise, and handsome. They also made sure to share Yahweh was with him. The wording for "brave" is an interesting choice, though, because it translates from the Hebrew phrase Gibbor Chayil, which is synonymous with "mighty warrior" and "person of significant social stature."[4] This further shows how people had begun to recognize him as God's chosen.

How does the biographer describe David's early relationship with Saul in 1 Sam 16:21-23?

Can you imagine how much David began to learn as a result of his new work? The God we serve is strategic.

What do you feel God has anointed you to do? What dreams has He placed in your heart?

How could your current line of work and ministy be preparing for the future?

Opportunities to serve the Lord come in greater ways every day. When they do, it is our job to remain cautious and ensure that we are not confusing the opportunity to help others grow in intimacy with the Lord with an opportunity to gain influence.

In chapter seventeen, we learn that Saul and the Israelites were fighting the Philistines. Why does the biographer keep mentioning Saul's name? Who should have gone out to fight Goliath?

What do you remember about Saul's appearance (1 Samuel 9:2)?

What caught David's attention and enraged him about Goliath in 1 Samuel 17:26?

Christian missiologists, E. Randolph Richards and Richard James point out that Saul's insistence that David wear his armor most likely resulted from one of two desires, or both:

1. Saul wanted the Israelites to think it was him on the battlefield since he should have fought against Goliath in the first place.
2. Saul could have proved that no one could have won against Goliath when David failed, wearing Saul's armor.[5]

Who did David say he would be fighting Goliath in the name of? (1 Sam 17:45) What would the assembly learn as a result of the battle? (1 Sam 17:47)

I've always found it quite curious that Saul asked Abner, his commander, whose son David was after he had David brought into the palace and asked Jesse's permission (1 Sam 17:55). However, it simply shows that there are people in your life who won't recognize who you are until God's perfect timing reveals it. Trust His timing. **Your obscurity is not a punishment, and neither was David's.** It was protection because from that point forward, the more success David enjoyed, the more suspicious Saul became of him. Saul continued to promote David, but we find that everyone who promotes you isn't necessarily your proponent. A proponent is an advocate, someone who is in favor of you, but Saul only promoted David because his own popularity grew as a result.

SESSION TWO

Lesson 4

1 Samuel 18-20

I failed miserably every time I attempted to read the Bible straight through as a teenager and then a college student. I just didn't get it.

It wasn't until I started reading the Gospels—Matthew, Mark, Luke, and John—that I began to read the Bible with a hunger to know more. I went through the entire New Testament, and then I doubled back and started reading the Old Testament. It was like someone had turned a switch on. It suddenly all made sense, and everything (the good, the bad, the boring, and the beautiful) pointed to Jesus. Jesus stated that all of Scripture speaks of Him, and it suddenly seemed like they did (Luke 24:27, 44).

It is clear that David was a type of Christ. There are multiple instances throughout his life that point to our Lord and Savior. However, he is not the only one whose life points to the coming Christ. Jonathan played a prominent role in history through the humility he chose to show, and his life points to Jesus, as well.

Write down what you already know about Jonathan:

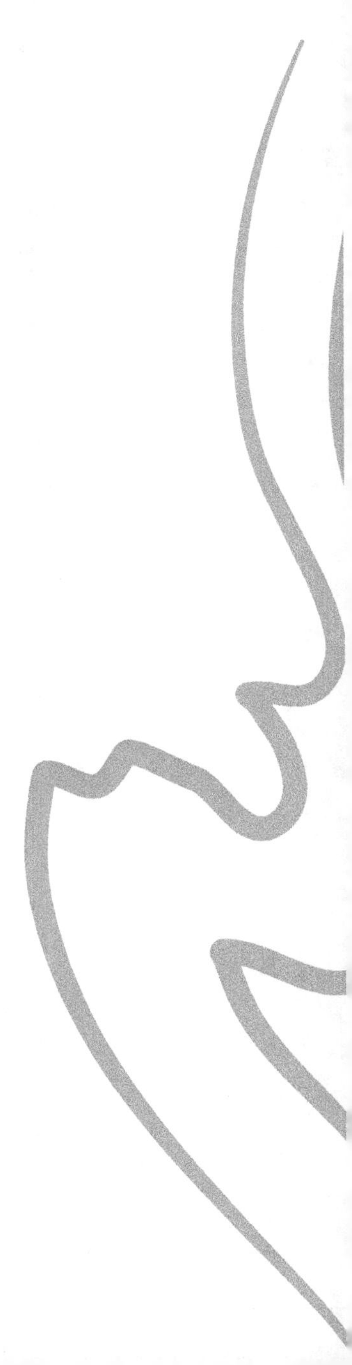

I can't think of anyone who serves as a friend more powerfully in all of Scripture than Jonathan (other than Jesus). We already learned that Jonathan was a man of integrity, acquainted with God, and influential among the Israelites, but here we discover that he was also a sacrificial friend who would give everything for God's will to succeed. When he and David entered into a covenant, he had everything to give and nothing to receive in return.

A covenant is different than a contract.

	Contract	Covenant
Obsolete when 1 party defies the agreement	✓	
Exists for the lifetime of the individuals, even if one passes away		✓
Allows recompense if one party breaks the agreement.	✓	
Remains effective even when one party breaks the agreement.		✓

Covenant is a big deal. We often conflate covenants with contracts, but when we do, we fail to capture and communicate the gravity and grace unique to a covenant. When David and Jonathan entered into a covenant, it was evident that Jonathan was the stronger party. Yet, he humbled himself to surrender to the presence of God in David's life. The Lord led David and Jonathan to love one another as they loved themselves, and we don't have to grow suspicious about their relationship because that is what the Lord has always instructed us to do.

What phrase do you see repeated in Leviticus 19:18 and Mark 12:30-31?

In 1 Samuel 18:4, we read that Jonathan took his robe off and gave it to David, along with his weapons. This was much more than a mere exchange of clothing. Scripture repeatedly shows one's coat or robe as synonymous with status.[1] Jonathan gave David his royal garments and weaponry to signify how much he honored David in front of everyone else. However, it also showed that he was willing to surrender his status and right to rule the kingdom, as well. It literally established David on equal footing with him.

The biographer contrasts Jonathan with his younger sister, Michal because we also learn that she loved David too.

Who was Michal (1 Sam 18:20)?

Michal's father consistently manipulated her affection for her husband. What did Saul require David to accomplish in order to earn her hand in marriage (1 Sam 18:25)?

Because Saul had evil intentions about his daughter's marriage, it frightened him that she loved David so intensely. How did Michal help save David's life (1 Sam 19:11-15)?

Unfortunately, Michal's love for David is contrasted with Jonathan in the text because when given the option, she chose to elevate her protection above her pursuit of God's presence. How did she lie to her father (1 Sam 19:17)?

Rebellion and idolatry influence us to fall prey to manipulative tactics and approval-seeking behaviors, and my heart grieves for Michal. In the desperation to kill David, Saul completely overlooked the household idol Michal had reached for (1 Samuel 19:13). Unfortunately, it is likely the case that she had picked up her idol more than once before.

The Hebrew word for idol is tᵊrāp̄îm, and even though it's translated into English as family idols or images, it is also the plural form of the rāp̄ā'. If you've ever heard God called Jehovah Rapha, you know this particular name of God means the "God Who Heals." There's something in a name. This connection is important because it shows us that even though Michal wasn't calling on Jehovah Rapha, she was looking for healing.

One of the most intriguing accounts of idolatry worship in the family of Abraham will forever remain the time Rachel took the idol from her father Laban's house in Genesis 31:34. Think of the correlation between that story and Michal's. It is possible Michal held on to this household idol like Rachel held on to her miniature one: to cure her infertility, though the Bible offers no clarification. Some commentaries draw comparisons between the idols Rachel took from her father, Laban's, house in Genesis 31:19, 34 and Michal's household idol.[2] Although we do not know why Rachel stole Laban's idols or Michal practiced idolatry, there is a possibility that they could have thought doing so would benefit their families.[3] The Enduring Word Commentary specifically points out that Michal could have used the idol for fertility support,[4] and we know that Rachel struggled with similar problems although she'd birthed Joseph.

What is most troubling is that this little issue that was once able to fit under Rachel's garments had grown into a life-size problem during Michal's lifetime when it was left unattended throughout the generations.

Isn't that sin's effect?

Sin intensifies when it is left unchecked, and Michal's idol was now so large it was mistaken for David at first glance (1 Sam 19:13-14). It was no wonder Michal chose her father's side. As someone who struggled with infertility for years, this breaks my heart. Still, the true tragedy is that idolatry grows with each generation that follows when they're overlooked and ignored.

Michal struggled with a generational curse. Exodus 20:5 informed the Israelites that if they bowed down to other gods and practiced idolatry, their descendants to the third and fourth generations would suffer the consequences. Michal was a direct descendant of Rachel because her father was a Benjamite, a son of the tribe of Benjamin whom Rachel bore (Genesis 34:16-18, Samuel 9:1).

Benjamin was blessed by Jacob, and Michal was much further removed from Rachel than the fourth generation. Still, she was a victim of idolatry when her father chose rebellion against the Lord (1 Samuel 15:23). The Word tells us she grabbed the household idol, and I feel for her because it clouded her judgment when faced with further challenges from her father, cutting her off from the healing that she could have found in the Lord's presence.

Idols steal the best of us, our relationships, and our future. They influence how we look at our world, love people, and lead others. There is no limit to the ways that idols take over our lives.

What kinds of things have your coping mechanisms been keeping you from?

Thankfully, we don't have to suffer the same trauma Michal would go on to endure. Galatians 3:13 tells us that Christ redeemed us from the curse of the Law by becoming the curse for us. It doesn't matter what curses have been spoken over you or how many evil entities you have agreed with in the past. Once you repent and give your life to Christ, He renews your mind and restores you to right relationship with the Lord. That's good news!

Although generational curses have been broken in Christ, we still struggle with generational issues. What generational issues do you recognize with your family? Ask the Lord to renew your mind in those areas.

Michal ultimately chose to betray her allegiance to her husband, but Jonathan honored his covenant and aligned himself with God's chosen. If there is anything that we can learn here, it is that entitlement and sin distance us from our ability to engage without a God-given purpose effectively. Michal felt entitled to convenience. Jonathan, however, chose to engage the issue. Agreeing to intercede for David and expose his father's intentions, he acknowledged that it may not end well for him. In one act of surrender, he laid down everything he was entitled to as future king: the kingdom, his hopes, his dreams, and his life.

Jonathan declared, "May the Lord be with you as he used to be with my father" (1 Samuel 20:13 NLT). How was the Lord with his father? The Lord was with his father when Samuel described Saul as the hope of all Israel. Jonathan knew David was meant to take his place, and he surrendered his rights completely. Jonathan reminds me of Jesus. Jesus left heaven to humble himself for us.

Meditate on Philippians 2:5-8 and write down any similarities that come to mind between the Jonathan and Jesus.

Who might God be calling you to be a friend like Jonathan for?

When was the last time you went out of your way to do a good deed or sacrifice something to show up for a friend without expecting anything in return?

Lesson 5

1 Samuel 21-22

I don't know about you, but I am adept at making excuses. There's only one problem: excuses undermine God's plan for us. They defy the fact that God is able to deliver us despite our difficulties.

I am ashamed to admit I have caused church hurt. Author and Pastor Jerome Gay, Jr., defines church hurt as the pain inflicted by religious institutions, their members, and their leadership, which results in their distance from God and others.[1] As someone who consistently prioritized the mission of getting the message of Christ out to larger audiences of youth, I often moved past others at a breakneck pace. My pace resulted in many careless words spoken at the expense of the very people I loved, and I failed to see it. The department I served enjoyed success, but I often attributed our internal issues to warfare, which wasn't completely accurate. It was not until I stepped down from leadership at the prompting of the Holy Spirit that I finally slowed down enough to see where my priorities were misaligned. The external pressures I felt caused me to view people as if they were expendable, and as a result, I failed to take accountability for the areas I should have assumed servanthood.

I tell you this because God has lovingly restored the relationships with those I once led. Although our relationships have shifted with new seasons of life, additional ministry opportunities only became possible when I stopped making excuses and started accepting responsibility.

What mistakes have been interfering with your peace lately?

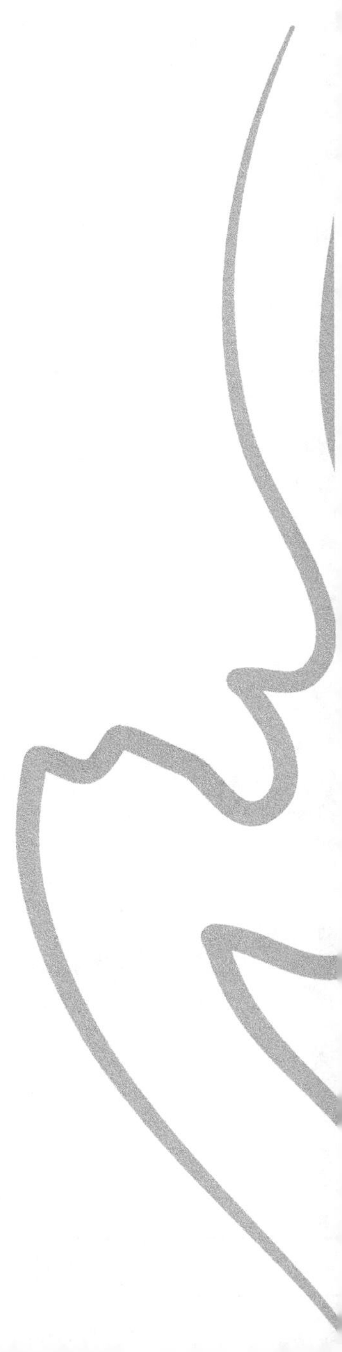

Worship is a gift because it helps us recognize God can redeem anything, and it serves as a practice to help us renew our minds. After all, we are not our mistakes. That one little fact helps us find the freedom to believe God's Word when our emotions say differently. It even leads us to stop making excuses about our part in the matter.

Worship leads us to face our issues head-on, to take responsibility instead of making excuses, and to acknowledge God can use the good, the bad, the ugly, and the beautiful despite our ability to ignore the problem.

So how do we make restitution? We repent. Worship should produce more than lip service. It should lead to an abrupt change in the direction you have been headed. Nevertheless, it will require you to incorporate other accountability matters that you adhere to as well.

Repentance is often reinforced through the spiritual practice of confession so that you can remain committed to the new directions. Regardless of what you think about confessing, we will find the more we practice it, the more conviction we feel. The opposite is true as well. **If you stop confessing your areas of weakness and opportunity for greater accountability, you will find compromise is closer than you realized.**

Once David left his meeting with Jonathan, he headed straight for Nob where the priests served. What did David take from the tent (1 Sam 21:4-6)?

Jesus would later reference this very incident in response to the Pharisees' accusations that Jesus' disciples didn't honor the Sabbath in Matthew 12:1-8. David and his men violated the law in Leviticus 24:5-9, and Jesus used the point to teach that the Sabbath was created for man. God has always desired mercy and the knowledge of God more than sacrifice (Hosea 6:6). It was through David's life that this principle is depicted over and over again. Still, Jesus used this point to prove that He was Lord over the Sabbath as He exposed the Pharisees hypocrisy. It is important to recognize that nowhere do we read that Jesus endorsed David's actions that followed, though.

One of the most important things we learn from David's life is that God called him a man after God's own heart long before he ever made a mistake, and not once did He regret giving David the kingdom as He did Saul. We are prone to think that this was because David was perfect, but that couldn't be further from the truth.

What did Doeg the Edomite do to gain Saul's favor (1 Sam 22:9-19)?

When Abiathar escaped, David didn't offer excuses. Instead, he accepted responsibility. By admitting he saw Doeg the Edomite spying on him that day, he acknowledged that he prioritized his purpose of escaping above the very people he was meant to protect.

Worship invites us to accept responsibility and repent of our mistakes. Worship is powerful because it consistently leads us to prioritize God's voice and put everything in perspective when we focus on Him. Repentance frees us to receive God's direction anew.

What direction did the Lord give David in response to whether he should rescue Keilah (1 Sam 23:4) following his admission to Abiathar?

How did David's worship settle his men's worries?

Worship leads us to prioritize God's voice and put everything in perspective.

SESSION THREE

Worship Invites God to War

Watch the video teaching
Organize Your Thoughts
Read and Interpret the Text Each Day
Surrender The Areas of Concern that Rise Up
Humble Yourself to Hear What the Lord May Say to Your Heart
Identify Ways to Act on What You've Learned
Pray for the Lord's Guidance and Protection

Watch the Video Teaching By Accessing It Through This QR Code

Organize Your Thoughts

The Scripture That Resonated with Me Today

Thoughs that Come to Mind and Prayers From the Heart

SESSION THREE
Lesson 1

1 Samuel 23–25

I love birthdays. I go all out for my friends' birthdays when I can, and nothing brings me greater satisfaction than the opportunity to review old goals and make new ones. Looking back over the years, nothing stands out like the night before my twenty-fourth birthday. After taking a year off of dating, I was convinced I was going to meet my husband (insert eye roll). Besides, I had just stepped into a role to lead a ministry at the church, and I was closing on my first house. It felt right.

When I met a guy we'll call Phil, I was overjoyed. He accepted my lifestyle as a Christian even though he was not a believer, and he had everything else on my list. Unfortunately, time would reveal that Phil was not simply resistant to Jesus. He rebelled against everything Jesus stood for and was involved in a lot of witchcraft. I refused to see any of it, though.

Throughout the short time we spent dating, I continued to worship the Lord, and I can now see how far the Lord went to war for me. Leaders whom I had previously had very little connection with started to tell me they were praying for me out of the blue. Some even shared a word of knowledge the Lord had given them to speak to the areas of concern. Still, it was not convincing enough for me to leave the relationship.

Other leaders (I knew more closely) began offering unsolicited advice, a unique benefit among friends and family. They reminded me that anyone who truly accepted my life in Christ would respect the time I commit to formally worshiping the Lord at church. They informed me that I should speak with him about refraining from scheduling dates that overlapped with Sunday service out of respect.

Even though I felt the Lord was leading me to leave the relationship, I did not know how, so I continued praying. As soon as I started praying for an out, Phil started having more serious problems in his personal life. At one point, the luxury-car-driving-tailored-suit-wearing-gentleman even ended up getting arrested on his way to pick me up.

It was not until after we broke up that I began to understand half of what Phil had been involved in. Thankfully, it didn't matter what I got or didn't get. My Heavenly Father did. The more I worshiped Jesus, the more He warred for me, and He will do the same for you.

As we encounter Saul and David this week, we will begin to recognize how great God's power is in comparison to others when we press into His presence. Keep praying. Worship invites God to war on your behalf.

God can redeem anything. Having repented from his past mistakes, we witness how cautious David had become to avoid hurting others. How many times did David pray about going to Keilah (1 Sam 23:1-5)?

What compelled him to keep praying (1 Sam 23:3)?

What did David do when wondering if the men would surrender him to Saul (1 Sam 23:11)?

Why might the men of Keilah have handed him over to Saul after he helped them in 1 Samuel 23:12? (Reflect on 1 Samuel 22:11-19)

We read about En Gedi in 1 Samuel 23:29, and this was a special place, further proving the Lord's ability to protect and provide for His children. En Gedi means literally "the spring of the kid (goat)," and it is one of only two freshwater springs located on the western shore of the Dead Sea.[1] What could this reveal about God upon further contemplation?

In 1 Samuel 24:2, we read that Saul took three thousand chosen men from Israel when he learned David was in En Gedi. How many people joined David? (1 Samuel 23:13)

Why do you think Saul took so many men with him?

What did David do to Saul in 1 Samuel 24:3-7?

How would calling Saul "father" shame him (1 Samuel 24:11)?

Saul was effectively shamed for a moment, but unfortunately, it was not long-lasting. What did Saul admit when he "repented" to David (1 Sam 24:20)?

As we venture into 1 Samuel 25, we meet an additional figure who also lacked integrity in every way in the life of Nabal. How does the biographer describe Nabal in 1 Samuel 25:1-3?

Individualist cultures often overlook important themes in Scripture because our identity informs our reading of the text, so one of the things we do not want to miss is how cultural mores specific to collectivist cultures show up in the text. In North America, we tend to think that monetary or material gifts pass *to* each other because we belong to individualist cultures. Yet, those in collectivist cultures believe gifts flow among each other and strengthen the shared identity.[2]

The biographers of Samuel expected us to know strings were attached to gifts when they began to contrast David's integrity with Nabal's irresponsibility.

Why did David expect to be fed from the harvest? What had he and his men done for Nabal (1 Sam 25:6-7)?

Nabal didn't just disregard David's request. He insulted him. How did Nabal refer to David (1 Sam 25:10)? Who is he echoing? Why is it insulting?

Offended, David instantly instructed his men to strap on their swords. Who prevented David from acting on his anger (1 Sam 25:18)?

Christian author and speaker Lysa TerKeurst writes that by assuming responsibility, Abigail repented before David by asking him to forgive her, his female servant. She also redirected his anger to help him see all that was at stake in the future.[3] Talking to David in verse 29, Abigail told David that God would hurl his enemies away as if in the hollow of a sling. By using such a strong metaphor, Abigail invited God to trace God's faithfulness. Had he killed Nabal, other innocent people would have undoubtedly died, and the Law strictly forbade killing innocent people (Exodus 23:7). He could have lost his opportunity to rule. Abigail told him not to pay any attention to Nabal, and he wisely took her advice.

David acknowledged that it was God who sent her, and he lavished his gratitude upon her.

What kinds of things have been distracting you from the Lord's calling lately?

The next morning, when Abigail told Nabal what had happened, his heart froze. This more than likely denotes that he had a heart attack or a stroke.[4] He died ten days later, and David considered it vengeance from the Lord.

The Bible specifically tells us that Nabal, which means "foolish" in Hebrew, was drunk from his feast when Abigail returned that night. Why would the Bible tell us she waited until morning? What do we know about Abigail's character? Could the Lord have been avenging her as much as David? The biographers of Samuel consistently reveal how God redeems women throughout the Bible, but they do not elaborate on this point.

David took Abigail to be his wife, which was a blessing to her because without a husband during these times, she and her wealth would have been exposed to potential attack from other men who had heard of Nabal's death. If his own sheep weren't protected in the field, how much more insecure would his widow be to attack?

A lifestyle of worship is one of humility and sacrifice. Nowhere do we see that displayed more than through David and Abigail's life. **Worship moves God's heart to war on our behalf.**

How has the Lord protected you throughout the years?

WORSHIP MOVES GOD TO WAR ON YOUR BEHALF.

The Scripture That Resonated with Me Today

Thoughs that Come to Mind and Prayers From the Heart

SESSION THREE

Lesson 2

1 Samuel 26, 28, 31

If the biographer worked hard to depict David's integrity, he worked equally hard to detail the great lengths Saul's idolatry went to. Determined to kill the man who had been declared God's chosen successor, he continued to prioritize his pride above God's presence.

Read 1 Samuel 26:6-12. What did Abishai take from King Saul?

Where were those items located?

Why do you think the biographer paid so close to where the items were, in consideration to Saul?

Throughout these books, we have observed how David's leadership matured. The Lord continued to show David that He was with David, and the fact that God caused Saul and his men to fall into a deep sleep showed that He had ensured David's success.

Here, David gives us a glimpse into the idolatry that was still influencing Saul's reign. The people-pleasing we saw earlier on was still pressuring him, and David called him on it in verse nineteen. By challenging him to acknowledge whether it was the Lord's doing or the people's pressure, David required Saul and the people to own up to the deep rejection he suffered.

We'll come back to chapter twenty-seven, but for now, we're going to continue our discussion of Saul. Samuel had not visited Saul at all after his choice to reject the Lord in 1 Samuel 15:34, and we didn't even read that Saul honored his death. Furthermore, Saul had made little attempt to pray or inquire of the Lord at all in the time since Samuel left.

Unfortunately, when we quench the Spirit of God and resist His leading, we start our search for spiritual substitutions.

Saul had long since rejected the Lord. He only prayed because he wanted a response, not because he wanted to repent. In his rebellion, Saul attempted to manipulate God once more. As a result, God refused to answer.

In what ways have you sought God's hand lately?	In what ways have you sought God's heart lately?

Our holy God deserves more than a half-hearted attempt at prayer that is bent on manipulating His hand. Instead of choosing to repent and humble himself, Saul asked his servants to find a medium in 1 Samuel 28:7.

Did they have trouble finding one? What could this reveal about their character (1 Sam 28:7)?

Ironically, the witch of Endor didn't realize she was talking to Saul, and one wonders if the biographers of 1 Samuel are making fun of her by pointing out the irony here.

So what's the problem if the witch confirmed what Samuel had said earlier? The problem is the Bible strictly prohibited contacting the dead in Deuteronomy 18:10-13. Those who seek their dead loved ones are further deceived. Rather than communicating with the dead, the psychics were instead communicating with demons.[1] Leviticus 19:31 called those whom they communicated with *"familiar spirits,"* wizards and psychics or necromancers, but the problem with familiar spirits is they deceive you into believing they're comforting you to gain a stronghold in your life.[2]

Unfortunately, many people turned to the occult out of a fascination and a desperation to find comfort in the supernatural. It's sad that so many haven't found the same comfort in Christ, especially since connecting with demons only produces death, both spiritual and, in Saul's case, physical. Furthermore, we must develop a healthy view of the Holy Spirit so that we can discern who He is and what He is not.[3]

Today, people are more likely to believe that the devil exists than they are to believe God exists. Research demonstrates that fifty-six percent believe Satan to be an influential spiritual being, while forty-nine percent doubt God exists.[4] Therefore, as Christians, we must become more active in pointing others to the solutions the Lord provides above the attractions the enemy offers.

Saul chose to take his own life as a result of the "prophecy" he had received in 1 Samuel 31:5, and it was a tragic death for Israel's first king.

In our ability to exercise free will, we will always face opportunities to impose our will above the Lord's. However, the one thing that sets us apart from the demons who attempt to control and manipulate our will is our ability to be restored to the Father through the act of repentance in Christ Jesus. The eighth chapter of Romans starts off by telling us that there is no condemnation in Christ Jesus and ends by reminding us that neither angels, nor rulers, nor powers can seperate us from the love of God in Christ Jesus.

If you have ever turned to witchcraft in the past. All you have to do is accept responsibility and repent. At no point did Saul ever take responsibility for his actions, and his pride eventually led him to fall prey to fear. What freedom would have awaited him if he had?

Suicide is a recurring matter in 1 and 2 Samuel. Unfortunately, many still take their lives today. If you are struggling with feelings of self-harm, please consider how precious your life is to our Lord and get help. The number to the suicide prevention hotline is 988, and there is no shame if you find you need to reach out for help.

I have had to reach out for help from my counselors and community a number of times, as well. The Word declares we overpower the enemy by the blood of the Lamb and the power of our testimony (Revelation 12:11).

The Scripture That Resonated with Me Today

Thoughs that Come to Mind and Prayers From the Heart

SESSION THREE

Lesson 3

1 Samuel 31

Some have asked me if those who have committed suicide are saved, and I recently had a conversation with Dr. Naida Parson, PhD.

Please find the video at this QR code.

Thoughs that Come to Mind and Prayers From the Heart

Lesson 4

1 Samuel 27, 29

One of the most beautiful things David teaches us is how much value and worth we have in the Lord. That lesson was no easier for David to learn than it was for ourselves. Because he's known as "the man after God's own heart," we often dismiss the hard parts of his story without paying a second glance (1 Samuel 13:14; Acts 13:22).

Rejection has a funny way of leading us to rebel when we lose focus on the fact that our worth is found in the Lord.

Before trailing Saul's tragedy in lessons two and three, the last thing David said 1 Sam 26:19-20, was that the people had forced him to go and worship other gods. Though a little dramatic, it was clear that he spoke out of great pain.

In 1 Samuel 27, David attempted to take up residence in an enemy nation. Unlike his first attempt, this endeavor, was successful. David had tried to settle in Gath back in 1 Samuel 21, but the men had reminded Achish who David was. Trapped and in trouble, David acted as if he was insane in order to escape. However, by the time he chose to go back to Gath in chapter twenty-seven, he was no longer afraid. It was clear he could aid the king. Why? Because David was no longer alone. He now led an army.

Where have we seen Gath before? (1 Samuel 17)

Here, we learn it's impossible to live in the enemy's territory and come out unscathed. We are bound to be influenced in some way, big or small. What did David and his men make a practice of doing in 1 Samuel 27:8-11?

Something counteractive is something that opposes, neutralizes, or mitigates an effect by contrary action. Although his work to assist God's people by working to eradicate the enemy all around did ultimately support the Israelites, the work clouded his judgment and led him to lose sight of his ultimate calling as the future king of Israel. Worse, it led him to strive after a role that was second best to the revelation His Savior had shown him.

In what ways have you caught yourself striving lately?

Why did Achish trust David? What had he been deceived into believing? (1 Samuel 27:12)

David showed his willingness to forfeit his very calling, and it's likely because he'd felt all of Israel had rejected him. However, it's here we learn that our calling is usually to lead among the very spaces that criticize and cast us aside.

What did Achish promise to promote David too (1 Sam 28:2)?

What did God promise to promote David too (1 Sam 16:1)?

It is possible that one of the reasons Saul became so fearful of this battle, in particular, was because he knew David was in Gath and supposed he'd be among the number to fight him. However, it seems important to note just how divided Israel—and even more, two prominent leaders in Israel—had become as a result of a refusal to worship God.

David offered Achish gifts from his spoils that were collected among the raids, and he addressed the king, calling himself Achish's servant.

What does the Bible say about having two masters (Matthew 6:24)?

As they prepared to battle the Israelites, the other leaders of the five major Philistine cities became alarmed that David and his men were following them. The Philistine leaders became enraged with King Achish for inviting David, and we see that Achish has been satiated by the spoils David has brought him. He had made no attempt to investigate David's claims about his raids.

Angry, the Philistine leaders demanded David and his men return to their post. They feared he might try to reconcile himself to his Lord.

When the Lord interrupted their plans and led the Philistines to reject him, David grieved it. Maybe it was all too familiar. After having experienced rejection from his own father early on (in 1 Samuel 16) and a father-like figure in Saul, he had finally found a leader who accepted and appreciated him. I can imagine it felt devastating, but it's often there in the middle of man's rejection that we find God's protection.

Access to Guided Prayer

WORSHIP REPAIRS OUR BROKEN RELATIONSHIP WITH THE LORD.

SESSION THREE

Lesson 5

1 Samuel 30

Although consumed by grief over Achish's rejection, David had not yet hit rock bottom. When David and his men returned to Ziklag, they found it burned to the ground. Their wives and children had been taken captive by the same Amalekites whom the Lord had wanted to protect Israel from during Saul's reign (1 Samuel 15).

What did David do when the men talked about stoning him (1 Sam 30:6)?

What do you notice is different about how the biographer talks about God in 1 Samuel 30:6 compared to 1 Samuel 15:15, 21, and 30?

1 Samuel 15:15, God is referred to as:

1 Samuel 15:21, God is referred to as:

1 Samuel 15:30, God is referred to as:

1 Samuel 30:6 God is referred to as:

The word "strengthened" comes from the Hebrew word hazaq, and it is also defined as "repair."[1] **Worship repairs our broken relationships with the Lord, and the more David worshiped, the stronger he felt.** In fact, the next thing he did was instruct Abiathar to bring him his ephod (or prayer shawl). With the ephod, he inquired of the Lord if he should pursue the Amalekites. The Lord, always ready to guide us when our repentance is genuine and sincere, answered him favorably.

What did the Lord say to David in 1 Samuel 30:8 in response to his question?

David did just as the Lord said, but only with four hundred men (two hundred stayed behind). What does the number of men who accompanied David into battle reveal about God?

When we see David and his men with the Egyptian, we see that David had returned to his senses. Rather than treat the man harshly, they fed him and then made a pact with him in return for his intelligence about where the Amalekites were camped.

The Lord led David to recover everything that was captured, and David began to act as the merciful king he would grow to be. What did the men who went to battle demand upon returning in 1 Samuel 30:23?

David taught his men that all, regardless of status, were essential to the mission. Both those who went into battle and those who stayed by the baggage were important.

We see the full restoration worship offers when David sent his spoils to the elders in Judah this time, in contrast to King Achish to whom he'd formerly been sending them. This time, he sent his spoils to the right people. **Worship holds the power of restoration and recovery when we accept responsibility for our past mistakes.**

In what ways have you discovered restoration through worship lately?

The Scripture That Resonated with Me Today

Thoughs that Come to Mind and Prayers From the Heart

PART TWO

Second Samuel

SESSION FOUR

Worship Invites Renewal

Watch the video teaching
Organize Your Thoughts
Read and Interpret the Text Each Day
Surrender The Areas of Concern that Rise Up
Humble Yourself to Hear What the Lord May Say to Your Heart
Identify Ways to Act on What You've Learned
Pray for the Lord's Guidance and Protection

Watch the Video Teaching By Accessing It Through This QR Code

Organize Your Thoughts

The Scripture That Resonated with Me Today

Thoughs that Come to Mind and Prayers From the Heart

SESSION FOUR

2 Samuel 1

There's nothing like a good cry. It is truly one of the ways the Lord leads us to greater healing and renewal, and I am always grateful for it. Nonetheless, that has not always been my story.

For years, I despised my emotional ways. I dismissed my emotions countless times, understating my unique opportunity to empathize with others in their pain and discomfort. Now that I know differently, I relish the opportunity to sit with others in their times of need, even as I feel the invitation to take my needs and my emotions to the Lord more freely. God's presence gives us the freedom to feel *all the feels*, as we recognize He is faithful to show up in all of it: the good, the bad, the ugly, and the beautiful.

I wanted to feel excitement as I looked through the immense windows of the rustic cabin my husband had rented to celebrate a project I'd completed. However, exhaustion blocked my ability to enjoy any of it. My husband noticed it and recommended we pray.

Time he put his hand on my back, I broke as if I were a crumbling dam, unable to prevent the waters from overpowering anything in its path. I cried for what must have been an hour. Tears of exhaustion, broken friendships, and unmet expectations continued to flow all weekend long. Yet, when we prepared to drive down the mountain at the end of the weekend, I felt oddly refreshed.

That trip was unlike any other. Because of the high elevation, I found it had become increasingly difficult to do simple things like walk or sleep. The altitude had affected my ability to breathe naturally, and it seemed to be as spiritual as it was physical. It was there that I learned the breathing exercises we use to navigate grief in between the tears can help us worship as deeply as the most heartfelt song. Focusing on our breathing in seasons of intense pain can help us to will ourselves to focus on God's will, in spite of our pain.

YWHY is one of the names of God we read about in the Bible. It is made up of aspirated consonants which means you release puffs of air when you say them, and the name YWHY sounds like breathing. Sometimes worship simply invites us to breathe.

Acknowledging the grief I felt helped me understand the reality that God is always ready to walk through it with us. Worship invited me to reconcile the differences between what I had expected and what I had endured, but it also led me to see God was with me in all of it.

Worship invites renewal when you make the choice to keep breathing and believe that God is yet at work in the middle of the grief. It helps us reconcile our differences with the past.

When we fail to reconcile our differences, we often idealize or demonize the past and reject God's sovereign plan by refusing to embrace what He's currently doing.

The book of 2 Samuel starts off every bit as heavy as 1 Samuel ended, but these two books were originally written as one, so the story simply continues. **Nevertheless, heaviness is bearable when you remember to breathe.**

On the third day, after David and his men had recovered their wives and children, an Amalekite messenger came to David to share what had happened to Saul and his sons. The Amelikite, an alien resident living in Israel, showed signs of mourning. However, his reasons for being on the battlefield cause us to grow suspicious.

Who was David fighting at Ziklag (Recall 1 Samuel 30:18)?

What did the Amalekite messenger say had happened to Saul (2 Sam 1:4-10)?

Had the Amelikite been telling the truth, that would have been tragic in itself, since the very thing God ordered Saul to kill could have ended up killing him. However, the Bible confirms that the Amelikite was lying in 1 Chronicles 10:4 by telling us that Saul died by falling on his sword.

As a resident alien in Israel, the Amelikite would have learned not to kill innocent people, but instead, it seems like he expected a reward, much like Doeg the Edomite, who killed the priests.

Even though he was lying, he received the same consequence a killer would have received. David ordered the Amelikite messenger's execution, setting a precedent for his reign.

David sent two messages to Israel by convicting the Amelikite. What were they?

We notice a clear set of priorities outlined in verses 11-16 when the biographer pauses to tell us how David responded to Saul's death What were David's priorities? Rank them here, "1" being most important.

_______ Rewarding or Responding to the Amelikite

_______ Leading the Israelites under his care once Saul passed

_______ Mourning his king and best friend

David demonstrated he was ready for a new level of leadership as one who prioritized God's approval above other people's attention and applause. That was something Saul never learned, and it was the very thing that almost took David out just days earlier. Thank God he recognized how to return to worship.

How would you describe your decision making skills? Do you find yourself preventing or reacting to problems more often? How would you benefit from taking time to slow down and process the decisions you face?

Create a decision making map that will help you slow down before you make your next decision.

Access to Guided Prayer

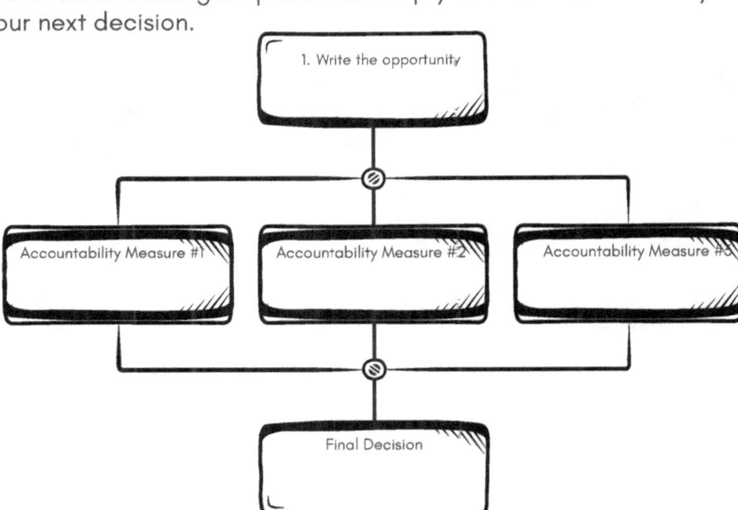

Worship invites renewal.

SESSION FOUR

Lesson 2

2 Samuel 2-4

Throughout the books of 1 and 2 Samuel, the biographers offer consistent insight into David's success: prayer and worship. These two spiritual disciplines secured David's position, dating back to his boyhood when he fought Goliath, and it would continue to be his secret weapon.

What did David do before leaving the Philistine territory and traveling to Judah (2 Sam 2:1)?

Where did David become king first (2 Sam 2:3-4)?

What indirect message did David send to Saul's most loyal subjects in Jabesh-Gilead when he blessed them (2 Sam 2:5-7)?

Who did Saul's cousin and commander, Abner, install as king instead (2 Sam 2:8-10)?

How long did the Israelite kingdom remain divided (1 Sam 2:11)?

Although honor killings were a common characteristic of collective cultures at the time, they continue to perplex those of us who belong to individualist cultures today.[1] Richards and James point out that the honor killings consisted of three components:

1. One party challenges another.
2. The challenged party responds.
3. The court of reputation weighs in.[2]

Who does the biographer describe as being more honorable in verses 12-32 (specifically, 17 and 31)?

What made Abner vow his allegiance to David (2 Samuel 3:1, 3:7-9)?

When Abner reached out to make a covenant with David, David agreed with the stipulation that his first wife, Michal, be returned to him, and Abner acquiesced. The Bible doesn't spare any details when it shows how many casualties Israel suffered due to King Saul's rebellion and the dissolution of the nation. Although difficult to read, I appreciate that the Holy Spirit inspired the biographer to include details about how hard this transition was on some of the women. **The text continues to clarify: God cares about women.**

Write down what you remember about Michal.

Saul had never considered Michal's marriage anything more than a plot to kill David. He only agreed to give her to David because he thought she would help him trap David, and he'd become even more afraid of David when he realized how much his daughter loved him (1 Samuel 18:21, 28-29).

We often read stories of the abuse of women in the Old Testament dismissively, disgusted that it happened, and there is a temptation to do so when reading 2 Samuel 3:14-16. A woman was being returned to her first husband as if she were part of the spoils of war. Meanwhile, the second man with whom she lived for over seven years (likely eight or nine years) followed her, grieving his loss. It's a grim picture, and the biographer's writing demonstrates that El Roi, the God who Sees, loved her enough to require others to pay attention to her pain, too.

Father wounds are found in the Bible. While traumatic, I have talked to women who have experienced significant healing through worship. Christian author and communicator Kia Stephens outlines a process to help women walk through forgiveness in her book Overcoming Father Wounds. Stephens reminds women that forgiving your father can open up areas to release greater healing in other areas you may have overlooked, as well.[3]

What about Michal's story resonates with you? Have you ever opened up about it to anyone?

With Michal having been returned to David, David hosted Abner, where Abner agreed to make David king over all of Israel. However, the drama had not yet subsided.

What did Abner promise to do for David in verses 20-22?

Why was Joab angry with David once he returned (2 Sam 3:22-25)?

Unfortunately, Joab caused David more pain and inconvenience by killing Abner. David, who worked tirelessly to reunify a kingdom, had to host a national funeral to distance himself from the assassination.

What did the sons of Rimmon, Baanah and Rechab, do to Ishbosheth?

What do you think they wanted in return (reference David's reward for bringing Goliath's head to King Saul in 1 Samuel 17:25)?

What do the similarities in the accounts of the Amelikite messenger and Ishbosheth's assassins reveal about leadership?

These greedy men assumed they would be rewarded but received the opposite reaction.

David waited approximately fifteen years to be king before he was anointed over Northern Israel, and a total of twenty-one years to be king of all of Israel. However, the gift of worship helped him wait on the Lord. In return, the Lord subdued every threat against his reign and ministry, and he was finally anointed king of Israel in 2 Samuel 5:3.

The Scripture That Resonated with Me Today

Thoughs that Come to Mind and Prayers From the Heart

SESSION FOUR

Lesson 3

2 Samuel 5-6

David's first act as king was decisive. He cleared the land of the Jebusites and finished the work his forefathers had begun years earlier (Joshua 15:63; Judges 1:21). When he accomplished the task and captured the stronghold of Zion, he renamed it the City of David and moved his entire family there.

The Lord continued to war on David's behalf and ensure his peoples' success, and we see this clearly in chapter five. What directive did the Lord give David in 2 Samuel 5:22-25?

What lessons about spiritual warfare can you observe from this passage?

What strategy or spiritual practice can you identify that's important? Here are a few examples to choose from.

Feasting/Fasting   Bible Reading   Fellowship   Silence & Solitude

How might your spiritual relationship with God improve through this spiritual discipline?

This illustrates just how many battles are won when we worship, but David continues to show us that even the deepest worshipers have to continually surrender their pride in the presence of the Lord.

Coronations are not as popular in North America as they are for those who live in Great Britain. Nonetheless, King Charles III's ceremony was broadcast across the world, and many news outlets published information about the events leading up to the ceremony in May of 2023, as well. The ceremony was highly religious, and the coronation oil was even consecrated in Jerusalem months before it was ever used.[1]

Despite the number of religious traditions that were included in the coronation, the coronation was not met with disdain from nonbelieving citizens. Christianity Today reported that most citizens disregarded the service's sanctity and instead viewed it as nothing more than a spectacle they were looking forward to.[2] Consequently, many Christian traditions that were incorporated into the three-day ceremony failed to persuade nonbelievers to turn to the Lord.

Can you imagine the shock if, for example, King Charles III's coronation surpassed traditional expectations and became one big worship service?

That's what David did.

The Bible does not acknowledge the events in 2 Samuel 6 as David's coronation. After all, he was anointed as king a third time back in 2 Samuel 3. However, the symbolism of this great event would not have been lost on any of his contemporaries.

In a time when kings only planned significant events and celebrations to honor themselves, the first and only ceremony we read during David's lifetime was held in honor of the Lord. He used this time to remind the Israelites that, monarchy or not, it was God who led Israel. Now that is a man after God's own heart: a man after God's own heart whose plans to honor the Lord still fell flat in the face of pride.

Is it possible to honor and serve the Lord from a place of pride? Saul's life would seem to affirm that it is not (1 Samuel 15). How did Saul try to honor God and keep his pride?

Are there any areas you've attempted to serve the Lord but became distracted, performing out of pride instead?

What does the Bible say about pride (Proverbs 11:2, Proverbs 16:5)?

In 2 Samuel 6, we read that David gathered 30,000 men to bring the ark of God to Jerusalem from Baale-judah (also known as Kiriath-Jearim), where it had rested for decades. Although the Israelites put away their idols and turned back to the Lord under Samuel's leadership, neither he nor Saul attempted to relocate it.[3] Jeremiah 7:12-14 references the judgment against Shiloh, where the ark was originally located under Eli's leadership, so Scripture shows that it was razed by the Philistines in the battle of Aphek in 1 Samuel 4. Unfortunately, this reveals Saul's indifference to the Lord's presence throughout his forty-year reign. In fact, he'd left the ark in the city known for worship to Baal.[4]

When David chose to bring the ark of God, where His visible presence manifested on earth among His people,[5] into Jerusalem, it was a big deal. However, David and the men should have focused more on God's presence than on their wish to be used powerfully.

What does the text tell us they set the ark on? (2 Sam 6:3)

One of the men responsible for moving the ark, Uzzah, stuck out his hand to touch the ark, which was a well-known and absolute violation of the Law. Consequently, God struck Uzzah in anger, and he died.

Today, many of us lament this just as David lamented it then. However, God is both loving and holy, and as we discussed in the first session, He will never contradict Himself.

As theologian and author Phylicia Masonheimer states in *Every Woman A Theologian*, "If God is only holy and not loving, there is no hope for us, but if God is only loving and not holiness, my behavior doesn't matter, and I am left in my sin, hurting other image bearers."[6]

God's justice may not always seem fair, but He has a consistent, communicated standard for His people. In God's incredible mercy, He gave the Israelites a gift: the gift of His presence motivated by His love and His desire to meet with His people on earth. However, much like Adam and Eve in the garden, His people were given clearly defined boundaries to enjoy that gift. Those boundaries remind us that even though He has given us a way to meet with Him (even more freely in Christ now), we are not the owners but the stewards of the gift.

It's completely normal to be angry with God. The man after God's own heart was angry too. That anger ultimately gave way to frustration and fear.

Where did David leave the ark (2 Sam 6:1)?

The Lord isn't afraid of our emotions. In fact, He invites us to bring them to Him. David grew fearful of the Lord, and you can imagine how defeated he must have felt. He had assembled 30,000 mem for the ceremony and returned to Jerusalem empty-handed. It was a loss that hurt David's pride. Thankfully, God can use any emotion to draw us closer to Him, and it's interesting what got David's attention.

Read 2 Samuel 6:11–12. What emotion do you think inspired David to act?

Something happens when we grow complacent in our calling. We start recognizing others who have similar callings, and we sometimes grow jealous-jealous of:
- their ability to walk in a similar calling freely, without the intimidation or restraint we seem to feel,
- jealous of how the Lord is moving in their lives,
- jealous that they're partnering with God in greater ways,
- and many more variations.

However, author Jo Saxton says that sometimes, "jealousy is proof that your calling that is calling."[17] David had a calling on his life, one that invited him to remind the people how important it is to pursue the Lord's presence. The Lord used Obed-Edom to remind him of that.

How has your calling been calling lately?

What Excites Me	What Makes Me Jealous	What I Feel Called to Do

Don't stop there. Pray God would continue to bless their work and ministry. Ask Him to make you bold as you answer your calling and help you grow as a student among others who excel.

Worship leads to greater reverence and joy. We're not going to get everything we want in this life. Some of us may wonder why our lives are so hard. Nonetheless when we worship despite the regret, we grow in our ability to reverence the Lord, and joy results.

David finally brought the ark of the Lord to Jerusalem, rejoicing the entire way, and we realize the biographer makes a note of entirely different details the second time around. There is no mention of thirty thousand men, though they may have been there. There's not much mention of the musical instruments. Instead, we notice that the king was dressed as a priest, wearing a linen ephod over his robes. Furthermore, in contrast to the majesty and splendor we learned about during the first attempt, the second was a bloody mess. Second Samuel 6:13 tells us David sacrificed an ox and a fattened calf after every six steps, dancing and shouting as they brought up the ark into the City of David. Attention was effectively redirected from David's goodness (as the first attempt at a coronation seemed to suggest) to how great God is.

David and the musicians likely recited Psalm 24 as they entered the city gates,[8] and wouldn't that have been something to hear? Psalm 24:7-8 (KJV) celebrates God with these words:

> "Lift up your heads, O ye gates; and be ye lift up, ye
> everlasting doors; and the King of glory shall come in.
> Who is this King of glory? The Lord strong and mighty,
> the Lord mighty in battle."

In what ways have the consequences you once viewed as unfair led to unexpected growth and unparalleled appreciation for the Lord's discipline?

"Unfair" Consequences	Unexpected Growth	Unparalleled Appreciation

The Bible is full of love, joy, pain, and heartbreak, and my heart breaks for the young woman who had been severely traumatized. Meeting David outside before he blessed the home, Michal criticized her husband's worship. Her pain seemed to speak loudly. Unchecked, pain led to criticism, contempt, defensiveness, and stonewalling[9] between her and her first love.

Michal's failure to recognize the freedom we find in the presence of the Lord led her to despise David's indiscretion, and she publicly denounced his actions.

David, defensive and protective of his position as a worshiper of the Lord, retorted that he would dance before the Lord and dishonor himself even more. Some believe David made a prophetic statement here in light of our coming High Priest and True King, who would humble Himself unto death for us.[10] Either way, one can understand how it must have pained him to hear his wife criticize him after everything he'd been through.

David no longer pursued intimacy with Michal, and she had no biological children. She does, however, have spiritual children: women whose relationships are falling apart due to the intense trauma they've been through.

Worship can restore broken hearts and relieve unbearable pain. It leads us closer to the Great Healer, but we must first get honest about our feelings. Let's honor Michal by taking our journey to recover and heal from our hardship seriously. God is with you, and He sees you.

Access to Guided Prayer

SESSION FOUR
Lesson 4

2 Samuel 7-8

As David continued to prioritize the presence of the Lord, David
verbalized his desire to build the Lord a temple. Nathan, the prophet,
initially agreed.

What was Nathan's initial reaction?

We learn that just because something is good, holy, and honorable
doesn't mean the Lord has called us to complete it alone. Instead, He
may want us to partner with others who are accomplishing the task or
pave the way so future generations of leaders can continue. It can be
challenging to accept, but when we do, it glorifies God more than our
good works ever could.

What was the Lord's response to David's request?

However, God outlined a covenant that He had planned to make with
David.

A covenant is a binding agreement between two parties, and there is
usually a stronger party in the agreement between two parties, and
there is usually a stronger party. In exchange for honor, the weaker party
vows their loyalty. Furthermore, the covenant is known to exist for the life
of the individuals. The last part is that the covenant will remain in place
even if the other party fails to keep it.

When we're invited into a covenant with the Great I am, the One who
is the same yesterday, today, and forevermore, our Eternal God, we
can be sure that He will fulfill His part long after we've become a
vapor (James 4:14). Furthermore, when the omniscient God calls us to
a relationship with Him and invites us into covenant, He does so

knowing that it's not a matter of if we will fail to uphold our end perfectly but when. God chooses to share His honor with us, all in return for our loyalty.

And that is why God's covenant is such good news!

The Lord had established multiple covenants with Israel up until this point.
- The Adamic Covenant was established with all humanity through Adam and Eve in Eden.
- The Noahic Covenant was established to reaffirm the Adamic Covenant.
- The Abrahamic Covenant was established to restore a relationship with a chosen group.
- The Mosaic covenant was established to renew Israel's ability to meet with God and live according to His righteousness.

However, it was the Davidic Covenant that pointed out the unconditional redemption of humankind through Jesus Christ.

Reflect on God's unconditional love. What comes to mind when you hear unconditional?

In 2 Samuel 7:8-9, the Lord reminded David that it had been He who was with David and secured His success. David's success had not depended on his human effort of unconditional love. God then made ten I will statements that confirmed His promises to David from verses 9 through 15. Can you find them?

This covenant was unprecedented. Not once did the Lord say, "As long as you…" It wasn't based on anything David had done, and, thankfully, it wouldn't be dependent on that either.

This covenant was a natural symbol of what God would do on earth through David's descendants, as David later believed that God was speaking about Solomon (1 Chronicles 22:9-10). However, it was as natural as it was spiritual. The Lord was speaking of Yeshua (Jesus), who would one day come as our Prophet, King, Priest, and Savior and be known as the Root and the Offspring of David.

After hearing Nathan's prophecy, David sat in the Lord's presence. There, he worshipped the Lord as he recognized that it was all out of the Lord's kindness. He talked to the Lord about how He had redeemed a people unto Himself and acknowledged that it was all His work. That is to say: the Lord did it without any help from Israel.

Interestingly, David called on the name of the Lord God of Heaven's Armies, or Jehovah Tsebaoth (the Lord of Hosts), throughout 1 and 2 Samuel, and we get a glimpse into the lessons David has learned. **When you worship, the Lord wars for you**. He wars for your home and your heart.

It is no coincidence that the biographer went on to list David's military victories as the Lord continued to establish his reputation for justice and righteousness. We will continue to demonstrate the ways David shared his power by elevating others as leaders, through delegation in contrast to the overbearing manipulation people experienced under Saul.

What military victories stand out to you from 2 Samuel 8?

Worship leads to greater reverence and joy.

Lesson 5

2 Samuel 9

After a rather heavy week, we end on a lighter note. You may recall that a covenant exists between the parties for the lifetime of the individuals, whether both are living or not, and here, the biographers continue to show us how righteous King David was.

David remembered the covenant he and Jonathan had entered into in 1 Samuel 20:12-17, and he sought to fulfill his part of the agreement.

What did David ask in 2 Samuel 9:1?

The word "kindness" here in Hebrew is *khesed* and its beauty is lost in translation because we do not have an appropriate English word to capture the many shades within this one concept. Khesed connects goodness, kindness, faithfulness, mercy, and favor and encompasses each description all that at once. For instance, here, it's translated as the kindness of God, but in Psalm 23:7, it's translated as mercy.

Name a recent event where you were surprised by the Lord's overwhelming kindness and mercy.

Who was Saul's servant whom David called in 2 Samuel 9:2?

What was Jonathan's son's name (2 Sam 9:6)?

You may remember the biographers paused in the middle of the account about Ishbosheth's assassination to detail how Jonathan's son had become crippled in 2 Samuel 4:4. It was important to note that his son lived in Lo-debar, not Mahanaim, where his uncle was killed because he would have been more susceptible to assassination there.

Apparently, Mephibosheth had been crippled in both of his legs when he was about five years old. His nanny had picked him up so they could escape when they received the news that Saul and Jonathan had been defeated. Unfortunately, she dropped him when she was running, and his feet were crippled as a result.

As unfortunate as it was, Mephibosheth had his life, and he had been living quietly at Machir's house with his wife and his young son, Mica (2 Samuel 9:12). It's amazing what you'll find to be grateful for when you've endured intense pain.

Lo-debar is translated as a "pastureless place" located in Gilead. The term "pastureless" likely meant a crowded town with no room for animals to graze. My heart is encouraged when I read this account. We see that it doesn't matter how dismal or distressed our situation appears. God's design for our lives continues to direct our steps.

God can rescue you from the obscurity of a crowded place when you choose obedience.

Are there any areas you feel called to even though culture characterizes them as "oversaturated"?

How have you continued to pursue life in those places?

When Mephibosheth arrived at the palace, he lied prostrate before the king, likely fearful for his life. It doesn't seem as if David's excitement at seeing him eased his fears. It was customary for kings to kill off any direct descendants to the throne of the former dynasty for fear of future threats to the kingdom.[1] This may have been going through Mephibosheth's mind at the time. Thankfully, David encouraged Jonathan's son by telling him not to fear and informing him he was going to restore all of Saul's fields to him.

David did not just stop there, though.

David also invited Mephibosheth to eat with him at his table continually. In that collectivist culture, this was a big deal.

Mephibosheth would have experienced shame as one of Saul's descendants and as someone who was crippled. Yet, David showed him khesed. Although we fail to see the depth of the love David showed

Mephibosheth, it was quite absurd and scandalous for the time, which is probably why the biographer mentions Mephibosheth's crippled feet a second time in 2 Samuel 9:13.

Christian co-authors Jayson Georges and Mark D. Baker point out in Ministering in Honor-Shame Cultures that such treatment—sitting at the king's table continually—would have given Mephibosheth the same reverence as one of the king's sons.[2] David fulfilled his covenant to his best friend. They write that such a reversal of status from Mephib-osheth's self-described status as 'a dead dog to royal son would have even eclipsed David's own exaltation from young shepherd to king.

What was Ziba ordered to do in 2 Samuel 9:9-13.

There is no amount of warfare that can prevent you from accessing God's promises when you worship.

Access to Guided Prayer

The Scripture That Resonated with Me Today

Thoughs that Come to Mind and Prayers From the Heart

SESSION FIVE

> Worship Invites Resilience in the Wilderness

Watch the video teaching
Organize Your Thoughts
Read and Interpret the Text Each Day
Surrender The Areas of Concern that Rise Up
Humble Yourself to Hear What the Lord May Say to Your Heart
Identify Ways to Act on What You've Learned
Pray for the Lord's Guidance and Protection

Watch the Video Teaching By Accessing It Through This QR Code

Organize Your Thoughts

There is no amount of warfare that can prevent you from accessing God's promises when you worship.

SESSION FIVE

Lesson 1

2 Samuel 10

"Ms. Liv, there was a girl who used to sit at the back of the church and cry all the time. Sometimes, I wonder what happened to her."

Another nodded in agreement, "Me too."

I looked at the small group of girls I was mentoring at church that day with a furrowed brow, wondering what could have inspired this comment at a second campus years after the series of incidents they described had passed. I could only suppose that the Holy Spirit had redirected the conversation to help us go deeper, so I decided to answer them.

"That was me," I responded. "I'm okay now."

"What? No!" All the girls looked up, mouths agape, trying to think if they could place me.

"Was the girl wearing a sweatshirt and a hat?" I asked.

"Yea, she wore it, like, all the time."

"Yep, that was me. I'm okay, now. Thanks for asking."

My life radically began to change within two hours of my choice to accept a position in Las Vegas, and it only intensified with each passing day. Isolated from everyone and everything I knew, I began drowning in depression. I used alcohol to satiate it, but it just worsened it, as it had always done.

I was in the middle of the wilderness, but I did not stop worshiping. Although I lacked a real relationship with the Lord, the church felt like it was my only lifeline.

Thankfully, I stumbled across a church that let me cry in the back, unbothered, during Wednesday night Bible studies. Even though they didn't bother me, I could tell someone was praying for me. Something was changing. I threw away all of my bottles after church one day, and I even called a new friend in the parking lot of a liquor store I desperately wanted to avoid returning to a few months later when I was in need of

dire help. I had slowly begun to feel hopeful about the new possibilities in front of me.

During that time, I found that worship helped me grow more and more resistant to old temptations. Eventually, many of those old temptations even ceased to appeal to me at all. The time I spent with the Lord became more fulfilling, and it changed my entire life.

Although worship never removed the sting of the consequences I suffered as a result of some of the choices I had made, it did speak to me about a loving Father. The Word tells us that God loves those whom He disciplines, and I am now more grateful for that. **I found the wilderness to be a way back to Him.**

My worship has not always resulted in reconciliation among old relationships I care about. It did, however, restore me to a renewed relationship with the Lord and help me recognize His strength is perfected in some of my weakest moments when I turn to Him.

Worship invites resilience in the middle of the wilderness when we press past our issues in the Father's presence without fear of condemnation. Although it does not always mean that it will result in reconciliation with those whom we have hurt or remove the consequences of sin. Worship does restore you to the Lord and offer additional opportunities to partner with Him.

In what ways are you challenged to believe the Lord is still moving on your behalf?

True to the contemporary culture at the time, the Israelites continued to war against neighboring nations in chapter ten, and it's here that we see it intensify. It would continue to escalate in David's natural and spiritual life throughout our session. However, it proves the last statement from our previous session's reading all the more. **There is no amount of warfare that can prevent you from accessing God's promises when you worship.**

As aforementioned, spiritual warfare is the opposition we encounter from the Enemy that challenges our intimacy and authority in the Lord. Second Samuel 10 outlines Israel's war with the Ammonites, and David emerged victorious again. While Joab battled the Arameans, his brother Abishai battled the Ammonites. Though the Israelites continued to win, the enemy grew stronger until the king emerged. While we don't want to diminish the fact that this was a real war, there is a lot to learn about how we battle spiritual warfare here too.

What does Ephesians 6:12 say?

The enemy loves to divide us in an attempt to conquer us. It doesn't matter if it's an army as it was with the Israelites, a marriage, or a ministry team. Oftentimes, it may look as if you are fighting a different enemy, but the truth is you are really fighting the same one on two different fronts.

When the fight begins to overpower our loved ones, fellowship in Christ means supporting, encouraging, and fighting for them in prayer. It is not a sign of weakness to call for help. Joab and Abishai showed that it was. a sign of strength and wisdom to call in the reinforcement.

Who are the reinforcements you call in when intense spiritual battles start to siphon your strength (i.e. a trusted pastor, prayer partners, mental health professionals)

Pride isolates and interferes with God's work, but unity and humility emerge from the unapologetic truth about our weaknesses, and it is where the battle is won.

Access to Guided Prayer

The Scripture That Resonated with Me Today

Thoughs that Come to Mind and Prayers From the Heart

SESSION FIVE

Lesson 2

2 Samuel 11-12

On the outside, sometimes people view worship as a ritualistic practice toward a god who requires it for his ego. That is not true, as many of us know. Worship is a gift God offers to access His presence in spite of the struggles we endure on this earth.

Why do you think chapter eleven starts by telling us that David sent Joab off to war without him, even though the biographer specified that this was the time the kings went off to war (2 Sam 11:1)?

The Lord sent a warning through Moses in Deuteronomy for the Israelites, reminding them to be careful to observe the His commands:

> "Take care lest you forget the Lord your God by not
> keeping his commandments and his rules and his
> statutes, which I command you today, lest, when you
> have eaten and are full and have built good houses
> and live in them, and when your herds and flocks
> multiply and your silver and gold is multiplied and all
> that you have is multiplied, then your heart be lifted up,
> and you forget the Lord your God, who brought you out
> of the land of Egypt, out of the house of slavery."
> (Deuteronomy 8:11-14)

This was not a condemnation of wealth.

What was God concerned His people would do as a result of their wealth?

The Lord had given David great favor, and it gave Him pleasure to do so. However, just like we sometimes do when we succeed, David had grown complacent in areas he had once exercised caution.

Suffering from insomnia, David strolled on his roof and saw Bathsheba bathing in the moonlight, which posed the first problem. The fact that David could see her from his palace incriminated him from the beginning. Bathsheba's proximity to the palace indicated her family's position in the kingdom. Christian professors and writers Randolph Richards and Brandon O'Brien point out that proximity communicated importance at this time in similar ways that it continues today. Still, David became obsessed.

Seeing her, David asked a servant to inquire about her, and the servant responded with a question.

What question did David's servant ask him in answer to David's inquiry about Bathsheba? (2 Samuel 11:3)

Characteristic of his culture, the servant attempted to protect the king's honor and address David's interest and insensitivity at the same time through his question. Yahweh had specifically restricted Israel from coveting their neighbors' wives in Exodus 20:17, and the servant alluded to this in the question he asked. David ignored the insinuation and sent messengers to get her, meaning he involved multiple people in his sin. Even though he knew who her husband was, he showed that he had grown self-indulgent, apathetic, and entitled.

Uriah the Hittite was one of his most valuable men. The Bible names Uriah as one of David's mighty men,[2] yet David didn't hesitate to bring Bathsheba to him. In so doing, David effectively shamed multiple families at once. From there, it only intensified.

Bathsheba went back to her home after they had laid together, and this heaped additional shame on her because under God's law, men who had taken advantage of women sexually were required to take responsibility (Deuteronomy 22). Unfortunately, he did not make it right, which shows how he had begun to act more like a Mediterranean king than God's anointed one.[3]

That refusal led to his fourth problem: his attempted cover-up. Richards and O'Brien note that kings at the time would not have summoned soldiers other than their commanders unless they were going to be promoted or punished. As one of the thirty, Uriah was no courier. On the contrary, he would have been highly important to keep on the battlefield. He was a soldier who would have undoubtedly questioned why he was being called.[4] Uriah knew he was either attending his own promotion ceremony or his death sentence, and he was faithful and honorable to the end.

When David instructed Uriah to wash his feet, he was using the Biblical euphemism to direct him to sleep with his wife because feet were commonly known to reference male genitalia. Additionally, the gifts he gave Uriah hinted at a bribe. All to no avail.[5] Uriah publicly slept at the palace door, refusing to play along.[6]

When asked why David had not gone home, Uriah used indirect language to reveal that he knew what had happened.

Who did Uriah mention as being on the battlefield in David's absence?

What three things did Uriah say that he had to refrain from doing?

When Uriah refused to play along after David's veiled threat, David wrote a letter to Joab requesting Uriah stand on the frontline abandoned to ensure death.

Forced to carry David's burden, Uriah innocently carried the letter ordering his own execution to the battlefield and died as a foreign mercenary among several other Israelites. It was not God's will for Uriah to die on the frontline of the battle by David's orders, and that will be even more evident in the following verses we study. However, Uriah must have known how he'd angered the king, and he went back to battle anyway. Though he had less motivation to be on the battlefield than the king, he may not have believed David to be capable of such evil, so he honored his king to the end. In return, our King continues to honor him.

Read Matthew 1:6. Who is named in the ancestral line of Jesus?

[7]

Uriah's name means "Yahweh is my light," and although we're not sure of when Uriah acquired this name or whether he was given it at birth, one thing is true: the Lord accepted gentiles long before Jesus came on the scene in the New Testament.

Following the Lord doesn't always mean that things will turn out favorably. In what ways have you felt wronged or treated harshly because of your choice to honor the Lord?

Where are you in your forgiveness journey with this person or situation?

Is there any healing you need to seek from the Lord through the help of prayer, support groups, or counseling?

In Chapter 12, the Lord sent Nathan to talk to David in a parable. It is possible Nathan used a parable because he feared for his life. Parables would have been an acceptable and common form of speech in an honor-shame culture. More importantly, it would also have helped Nathan continue to honor the Lord. David had already proved to be ruthless with Uriah, and this may have offered Nathan additional protection. Furthermore, the parable would have appealed to David's sense of justice and empathy in spite of the fact it is possible he believed he'd done nothing wrong.

Either way, it worked.

Who was David in the parable (2 Sam 12:1-6)?

What consequences did Nathan prophesy David would endure (2 Sam 12:10-12?

What does this reveal about God?

David declared he sinned, which is as much a part of worship as our devotion. As a result, Nathan said the Lord had taken his sin away. Yet, the Lord did not take away his consequences. David would soon grieve the loss of several of his sons. Still, it was worship that carried him through. And that's exactly what he did when he learned the baby Bathsheba had borne had died.

Worship doesn't have any restrictions when it reveres our Lord. **It is in worship that we learn how to reflect on the goodness of God, even when we don't feel good.**

When David went in to comfort his wife, she conceived Solomon, which sounds like the Hebrew word for peace, *shalom*.

WORSHIP LEADS US TO REFLECT ON GOD'S GOODNESS EVEN WHEN WE DON'T FEEL GOOD.

SESSION FIVE

Lesson 3

2 Samuel 13

In all honesty, I sat with chapter 13 for weeks when I first felt the Lord leading me through these books. I couldn't move on because question after question plagued me.

Second Samuel 13 is a traumatic and heart-wrenching narrative of a young woman who was abused in the most heinous way. It reminds me of the painful events we read about during the time of the judges and Saul's reign. As someone who also has a history of abuse from a bad relationship gone wrong, I had to wrestle with this passage.

When presented with the choice to wrestle or walk away, remember worship always invites us to wrestle.

What scriptures do you wrestle with? How are you continuing to seek the Lord?

Our free will requires the need for a Holy God to help us understand what it means to honor Him and His image bearers. As image bearers of the Lord, we fall short of our responsibility to respect humanity when we fail to reverence God. If you are someone who has been abused or know someone who has, it is my prayer you would remember this is not a prescriptive passage.

God does not sanction rape. Ever.

This is a descriptive passage. It is here so we can see the events and their severity in light of the overall narrative. Even so, I believe it's deeper than that. This story reveals the depths of shame Tamar was subjected to, and doing so restores her honor. The Word tells us we overcome the enemy with the blood of the Lamb and the power of our testimony (Revelation 12:11). The story exposes how abusive her brother was, and it also directs our attention to how negligent David acted as a father.

The text is clear: Tamar deserved better.

Meditate on Revelation 12:11 in your personal Bible and reflect.

Is there anything the enemy has attempted to silence you about?

How will exposing it in truth, love, and prayer, as you follow the Holy Spirit's leading, help you to defeat the Enemy?

The Bible specifies that Absalom and Tamar, the children of King David, and their mother, Maacah (the daughter of King Talmai of Geshur), were very good-looking in multiple passages . The narrative then continued to say that their half-brother, Amnon, who was the crowned prince, loved Tamar. However, this was not innocent love.

The next verse tells us that his feelings for her tormented him, and it "seemed impossible to do anything to her" (2 Samuel 13:2 ESV). We're not sure whether this was because she was a virgin, which parallels this verse, or because she was a princess. Nevertheless, the biographer indicates Amnon did not have good intentions toward her. His use of language intensified as the situation unfolded.

Verse three tells us he had a friend named Jonadab. The New International Version even calls him an "advisor." This is important for two reasons. The change in the description across translations shows the connection between our friendships and the advice we welcome as a result. It demonstrates there are times when they're indistinguishable. Jonadab was Amnon's cousin, and the Bible describes him as a shrewd or crafty person. Although the word hakam can be translated as wise, the context here suggests a negative and evil connotation.

From the very beginning, Amnon's friendship with Jonadab was disconcerting.

Jonadab started asking Amnon questions, leading him to make an evil conclusion. I've always viewed this as a powerful depiction of Proverbs

6:16-19:

> There are six things that the Lord hates,
> seven that are an abomination to him:
> haughty eyes, a lying tongue,
> and hands that shed innocent blood,
> a heart that devises wicked plans,
> feet that make haste to run to evil,
> a false witness who breathes out lies,
> and one who sows discord among brothers.

Return to the scripture quoted above. Circle the traits Jonadab displayed in 2 Samuel 13?

Though Jonadab never suggested rape, his conversation helped Amnon conceive a plan to get Tamar alone, and it worked.

What did Jonadab tell Amnon to do?

How did Amnon get Tamar alone?

Although it was improbable that Amnon and Tamar would be able to wed on the basis of incest, Tamar did everything she could to dissuade her brother. Unfortunately, rape was only a part of the sin committed against her. Amnon's sin led him to hate her even more than he once supposedly loved her, and he continued to wrong her further.

Deuteronomy 22:28-29 detailed what should happen if a woman was raped, and although it might be appalling to us. scholars suggest it was God's way of requiring men to take responsibility for the crime they had committed and decrease the number of attacks against women.[1] A woman who was violated would have had no hope of a family and open to even greater vulnerability. It would have left her even more exposed and insecure financially and physically once her parents passed.

Although living or starting a family with the one who violated you was not ideal then or even imaginable to us now, this served two purposes. First, it would cut down the number of men who committed this crime, and secondly, it would require them to honor her for the rest of their lives. When Amnon sent Tamar away, he rejected God's Law, and he rejected Tamar, robbing her of her chance to live without public shame.

Amnon called the servant, had her thrown out, and ordered the door be locked behind her. Publicly shamed, Tamar began to mourn loudly, but Absalom calmed her down.

What reason could Absalom have for quieting her down?

What did King David do in response (2 Samuel 13:20-25)?

After two full years, Absalom began to scheme to take Amnon's life. He invited the king and his sons to the feast he was preparing in a plot to kill Amnon, and it is possible he was planning to kill David as well. David, however, did not believe it would be good for all of them to be[2] in one place and rejected the invitation. Whether he altered any possible plot against his own life is uncertain.

What indicates that King David was suspicious for Amnon's sake (2 Sam 13:26)?

Absalom's plot was successful. Chaos immediately broke out, and someone told the king the rumor that all his sons had passed.

Who reassured the king that all of his sons had not been killed (2 Sam 13:32)?

One is left wondering what Jonadab's motives were for stirring up so much confusion among the family. Could it have been to see some of David's eldest sons passed over and restricted from reigning as his father had been (1 Samuel 16:9; 1 Chronicles 2:13)? Only the Lord knows.

Think about who you listen to the most and whom you would identify as your inner circle. Start with three people and write their names on the inside of the circle. Move out from there, naming additional people whose advice you value, as well.

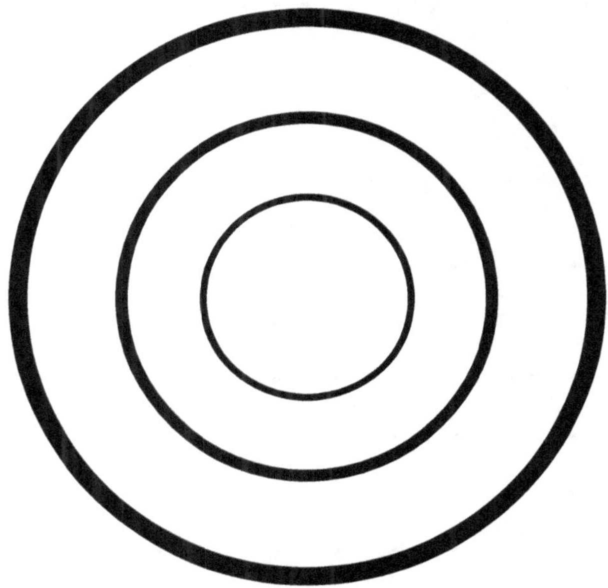

Does anything about this surprise you? Is there anyone you feel led to move to a different sphere within your circle based upon what their patterns demonstrate.

The Scripture That Resonated with Me Today

Thoughs that Come to Mind and Prayers From the Heart

SESSION FIVE

Lesson 4

2 Samuel 14

Absalom sought refuge in his grandfather's kingdom of Geshur after he ran, and he remained there as an exile until David stopped mourning for Amnon. The Bible tells us that King David began missing Absalom but did nothing about it (2 Sam 13:39).

Joab recognized it and decided to help the king reconcile with his son, so he called for a wise woman from Tekoa.

This woman is recognized as a respected diplomat in Jewish culture.[1] In the West, modern-day readers sometimes debate this woman's role and the impact she had on King David. Nonetheless, the Midrash, an ancient Jewish commentary, reports the wise woman of Tekoa was known as one of the twenty-three truly upright and righteous women in all of Israel.[2] She has a lot to teach us.

Tekoa, the town she was from, was situated on the southernmost border of the Judean desert, and it was approximately twelve miles from Jerusalem.[3] It is interesting that the commander called a woman from outside of Jerusalem to help the king reconcile with his son, but a further look into Tekoa reveals why he chose to do so.

Tekoa was located at a high altitude and was known for its olive trees. In ancient Jewish culture, olive oil was associated with wisdom, and the women who lived in the town had a reputation for being wise.[4] It made perfect sense to the Israelites reading the books of 1 and 2 Samuel why Joab would invite a woman from the town of Tekoa. We, however, have to dig deeper.

The woman who was called had an exceptional character and discerned how to approach the king. She also understood how to encourage and hold him accountable without ever shaming him. Joab told her how to dress and conduct herself, and he provided a dilemma for her to share with the king.

One of the reasons this woman is revered is not only because of her wisdom and intelligence, but also because of her courage:[5]

- She did not hesitate to appear before the highest leader in her land.

- She must have had skill at helping others in precarious situations, which is why she was chosen to help the king.
- She had developed sensitivity to the One from Whose Spirit releases blessing and wisdom.

Proverbs 9:10 reads, "The fear of the Lord is the beginning of wisdom, and knowledge of the Holy One is insight." Joab could get her access to the king, but her character would have to keep her there. And it did.

Are there any words you've been waiting to write or speak until you get a "bigger platform?"

What benefits could speaking and writing about the areas God has placed on your heart bring? Circle the following you believe apply, especially if you are having trouble writing an answer.

The opportunity to encourage someone

Greater knowledge and insight

Additional skill that flows from your obedience

Partnerships that will carry your message further

In what ways does her "dilemma" compare to Nathan's parable in 2 Samuel 12:1-7)?

King David gave her permission, and then she carefully and lovingly corrected him while offering encouragement at the same time.

How does the statement The Wise Woman from Tekoa made in 2 Samuel 14:14 prophesy about Jesus?

How does granting "Joab's request" help King David save face in light of what you now know about honor-shame culture?

The strength of the Wise Woman of Tekoa's character revealed her commitment to the right thing at all costs, overpowering fear and avoiding extremes.[6] The woman of Tekoa's character stands in contrast to King David's here.

King David allowed Absalom to return, acting as if it was a favor he was extending to Joab, but he initially refused to see Absalom, and this further distanced his son.

Absalom is consistently painted as a compassionate man who has a love for justice. We see this both in his treatment of his sister, the biographers' commentary about how loved among the people he was, and small details like the fact that he named his daughter after his beloved sister. However, we notice a shift when he set Joab's field on fire in 2 Samuel 14:28-32. Sadly, rejection often leads to rebellion.

Why did Absalom set Joab's field on fire?

What happened as a result (2 Sam 14:33)?

WHEN PRESENTED
WITH THE CHOICE
TO WRESTLE OR
WALK AWAY,
KNOW THAT
WORSHIP
ALWAYS INVITES
US TO WRESTLE.

SESSION FIVE

Lesson 5

2 Samuel 15-19

As we have seen through David's own life, rejection leads to rebellion unless we worship the Lord through it. The key is to *worship*. Unfortunately, Absalom chose to revolt instead.

What does Absalom do to take control of the kingdom in 2 Samuel 15? Fill in the blanks using the ESV translation in addition to what you wrote for the previous question:

a. After this Absalom got himself a ______________ and ____________ , and ____________ men to run before of him (v. 1)

b. And Absalom used to __________ early and stand beside the ______________ of the _________; ... (v. 2)

c. Then Absalom would say, "Oh that I were ______________ in the land! ..." (v. 4)

d. So Absalom ______________ the ______________ of the men of Israel (v. 6)

e. At the end of _________ years Absalom said to the king, "Please let me go and pay my vow, which I have vowed to the Lord in ____________" (vs 7)

f. The king said to him, "__________ _______ ____________." So he arose and went to ______________ (v. 9)

g. But Absalom sent ____________ __________________ throughout all the tribes of Israel, saying, "As soon as you ____________ the sound of the ____________, then say: ______________ is __________ at ____________!" (v. 10)

One significant shift in Absalom's rebellion came when King David's advisor, Ahithophel the Gilonite, joined him. If you remember, Bathsheba was the daughter of Eliam and the wife of Uriah the Hittite (2 Samuel 11:3). Eliam was Ahithophel's son (2 Samuel 23:4), which makes Ahithophel, Bathsheba's grandfather. This is important for two reasons. First, it signifies David had shamed two family names, and second, it shows an additional motive for Ahithophel's choice to aid Absalom. It's probable Ahithophel had chosen to join Absalom out of a desire to see David shamed for what he'd done to his grand-daughter and their family. His alliance with Absalom also gave Absalom greater credibility.

In fact, the biographer's statement that the "conspiracy grew strong," as well as David's choice to leave immediately, may also demonstrate the military was on Absalom's side, too (2 Samuel 15:12 ESV).

This scene illustrates how tragic many parts of David's life were. However, rather than gloss over them, the Lord moves the biographer to include the details so we can understand the depths of despair David endured in his life.

What did David do to protect the people who left with him 2 Samuel 15:18-30?

There, in the middle of the road to the wilderness, David worshipped by sacrificing to the Lord. Please note that English Standard Version is the only translation that does not include the statement that Abiathar offered sacrifices. David worshiped on the way to wilderness, and it was not lost on God. Contrary to Saul, who had attempted to manipulate God's hand in fear of his last battle, David chose to accept God's will. **Worship leads us to accept God's will even when we're on our way into the wilderness.**

Once all the people passed, David commanded the ark of God to be returned to the city, acknowledging his future was in God's hands and that he would trust Him completely. He even acknowledged that Zadok was a prophet and said they would wait for an answer. This difference continued to distinguish him from his predecessor when he faced destruction because character is proven in chaos. Whereas Saul consulted a witch, David consulted a man of God.

Prophets throughout the Bible do speak of the future. However, they deliver messages consistent with God's Word and ultimately lead people to worship the Lord God with greater intentionality.

Many people confuse psychics for prophets, but the Bible instructs that they are different. The word "seer" used in the Old Testament comes from the Hebrew word ra'a, which means "to have a vision, discern." In contrast, the words, 'ôb̲ and qāsam, used in translation that refer to the witch of Endor speak of necromancy and divination. The witch of Endor and Zadok the priest, were different, and the fruit they bore demonstrates that. Prophecy leads us to become more intimate with the Lord, whereas psychic readings and witchcraft lead to greater isolation from the Lord, regardless of how similar their gifts seem to be.

Romans 11:29 states that the gifts and calling of God are without repentance. It references the Jewish people's enemy state with God, showing that the gifts the Holy Spirit gives us are irrevocable. Therefore, someone who may have a prophetic calling can deny its purpose in the Lord and use it for evil, by rejecting the Lord and choosing, instead, to serve Satan. David's restraint and refusal to kill the "Lord's anointed" even when David was in great danger further proves this. David recognized that even though Saul had stopped consulting God, the fact that he still retained his position was proof that God had not yet stripped Saul's "gift" from him.

Today, we must recognize that although the same gift may exist in both prophets and psychics, the source makes the difference. Psychics do not speak for God. Neither do they bring peace in the middle of our problems by leading us closer to God. Instead, the peace they promise leads to greater isolation from Him. Demon possession is as real today as it was in Scripture.

David recognized the difference, and it brought contentment in the middle of the chaos. As a result, God's provision began to show up in the place David had previously enjoyed the Lord's presence.

What did Hushai the Archite choose to do in support of David (2 Samuel 15:32-37)?

Unfortunately, not everyone was as honorable as Ittai or Hushai, and some used David's pain as an opportunity to pursue promotion. Ziba proved treacherous and got rewarded with Mephibosheth's land and wealth. Shimei also took advantage of the moment to curse and shame David. David, however, accepted it as his correction from the Lord.

And there is some truth to that.

How did Absalom's actions in chapter 16:15-23 fulfill the prophecy spoken to David in 2 Samuel 12:11-12?

What did Ahithophel advise the king to do? (2 Sam 17:1-4)

How did Hushai the Archite advise the king? (2 Sam 17:6-13)

The Lord caused Hushai's advice to appear more favorable, saving King David. Notice how the biographer mentions another woman who played an integral part in David's victory, too in 2 Samuel 17:16-22. Similar to Rahab, who helped the Israelite spies hide centuries earlier under Joshua's leadership, this woman worked to hide two spies for King David in a well until the threat of danger had passed.

How many women can you name from the beginning of this study who played important parts in Israel's success?

Ahithophel knew Absalom's dynasty would not last, and he went home and hung himself. Please refer back to our conversation on suicide for greater context and encouragement.

Who killed Absalom (2 Sam 18:1-15)?

David mourned his son bitterly, and yet worship led David to see how God was with him in the wilderness. Although tragic and devastating, we do witness one beautiful reconciliation. Mephibosheth approached the king as he prepared to reenter Jerusalem with the true story.

What did Ziba do to Mephibosheth? (2 Sam 19:26-27)

Access to Guided Prayer

When David announced Mephibosheth, Jonathan's son, and Ziba were to divide the land of Saul, Mephibosheth said he was content with David's return. He did not show a desire for the land. **Here, Mephibosheth showed David the Father's heart: what we do for the Lord pales in comparison to who we are to the Lord.**

SESSION SIX

Worship Invites You to Rejoice

Watch the video teaching
Organize Your Thoughts
Read and Interpret the Text Each Day
Surrender The Areas of Concern that Rise Up
Humble Yourself to Hear What the Lord May Say to Your Heart
Identify Ways to Act on What You've Learned
Pray for the Lord's Guidance and Protection

Watch the Video Teaching By Accessing It Through This QR Code

Organize Your Thoughts

The Scripture That Resonated with Me Today

Thoughs that Come to Mind and Prayers From the Heart

SESSION SIX

Lesson 1

2 Samuel 19-22

The Lord's presence can feel elusive at times. There have been days that it seemed like more of a mystery or a myth than a meeting place with God. However, I now know His presence can manifest in:

- a dark closet where you have determined to take your life,
- a bed of depression you can't find the strength to desert on your own,
- and a dance floor in the most unlikely places.

Writing this study was intense, and I have faced countless storms. I have witnessed beloved dreams die, and others find new life. I have faced uncertainty and depression that is reminiscent of my earliest days as a young adult. I have cried and questioned if I could do this. Still, each time I questioned it, the message God spoke to me as I wrote this book grew louder.

Worship.

Life can feel stifling, threatening to suffocate the last bit of strength we have left, but it does not stand a chance when we worship. One of the first lessons the Lord ever taught me seems fitting to end this study with. Early on, the Lord showed me the need to prove people wrong about me was the wrong motivation.

Despite the forgiveness I attempted to offer those in my past who hurt me for years, I still withheld a little. It was the last morsel of chocolate mousse cheesecake I held on the tip of my fork to savor, and I planned to do just that. In fact, one day, it showed up in my prayers. My prayers sounded like the imprecatory psalms we read about that ask God to judge our enemies. I didn't really want Him to judge my enemies. I just wanted Him to help me prove them wrong until one day, He stopped me in the middle of the track at Nellis Air Force Base.

One sentence penetrated my heart, almost causing me to fall over my own feet: "It's time for you to get over that."

I'd like to say I was humbled, but I was angry at first. That thing the Lord was telling me to get over had been the one coping strategy that I had held onto to process the rejection I had experienced early on. I had developed it to get over the very rejection He had allowed me to go through, and it felt unfair to have to release it as an adult.

The Holy Spirit began to comfort me in that moment though, as He showed me He had more to offer. My obsession with my reputation restrained me from moving farther in His love. The Lord wanted to help me enjoy the unrestricted freedom that comes when we redirect our attention to His reputation. He wanted to turn my mourning into dancing of the sweetest kind:

- The kind you can only enjoy when you don't care if anyone notices you.
- The kind that keeps you smiling long after you have stopped.
- The kind that is meant for an Audience of One.

Worship Invites You to Rejoice in the Lord's Presence.

We have consistently seen that worship leads to repentance in 1 and 2 Samuel. Guilt is sticky, and it can create further distance between you and the Lord by making you feel unworthy. However, you weren't good enough to go before the King on your best day, which also means you're no less worthy to go before Him on your worst day, either.

When we worship, we are able to recognize the many ways God rescues us. The more we recognize the many ways God rescues us, the more naturally praise pours out of our hearts. God is our ultimate Redeemer, and our soul always finds protection in His presence. David knew that better than anyone.

In what ways have you felt the Lord rescue you before?

God redeemed the way women were viewed and the importance ascribed to them throughout the books of 1 and 2 Samuel from the very beginning. The Holy Spirit continues to draw our attention to the many ways God partners and pays attention to women right on through the end of these books. In chapter twenty, we meet another wise woman.

Who was Sheba and what tribe did he belong to?

Who also belonged to his tribe?

What did Sheba tell the men of Israel?'

Was he convincing?

What position does Amasa now have in the kingdom (2 Sam 19:13)?

Who killed Amasa?

Who offered to help Joab?

What did the woman promise Joab?

What characteristics did the woman have that convinced her community
to follow her advice?

What happened to Sheba?

IWhat does the Bible say about wisdom in Proverbs 1:7?

What are some of the blessings of wisdom that are named in Proverbs 3?

The Scripture That Resonated with Me Today

Thoughs that Come to Mind and Prayers From the Heart

When we worship, we remember the ways the Lord rescues us.

SESSION SIX

Lesson 2

2 Samuel 21

It never ceases to amaze me that God chose to partner with so many women to bring the nation of Israel to attention about the areas that concerned his heart. He continues to do it today among those who are drawing attention to the justice God offers through His love and holiness, just as He did it through Rizpah's sacrifice in David's life.

This story may be uncomfortable to read, but it stands in stark contrast to the book of Judges' final account about the treatment of women. There, the concubine's dead body had been cut into twelve pieces and sent to the twelve tribes as a demand for "justice" by the Levites. But here, the last story is about a woman who demands justice.

Biblical accounts include much information about the wars and battles fought between neighboring nations because violence was how people established dominance, secured partnerships, and expanded their borders (and it is still how some nations do so). What seems unnatural to us united them. Still, killing of anyone was never God's intention for humanity.

Israel had entered into a covenant with the Gibeonites when Joshua first led them to assume stewardship of the promised land (Joshua 9:3-21). Unfortunately, true to his character, Saul broke that covenant. He killed the Gibeonites, and when no one sought to correct the issue, God sent a three-year famine upon Israel in 2 Samuel 21.

What did the Gibeonites demand in return for the injustice committed against them 2 Samuel 21:4-6?

Leviticus 24:17-22 allowed this, so David handed over Saul's remaining descendants, with the exception of Mephibosheth, whom the Lord allowed to live so that David could keep his oath to Jonathan.

Though Saul had passed, and his influence was long overshadowed by David's, some people were still greatly affected by this. Rizpah was one of them. She was the same concubine Ishbosheth accused Abner of sleeping with in 2 Samuel 3:7-11. Although we don't know if the accusation was true, it is clear that the Lord wanted to make her righteousness known here.

Rizpah reminds me of the woman who appeared before the unjust judge in the parable Jesus shared in Luke 18:1-8. Through her life, we see that women continue to move the heart of God.

In 2 Samuel 21:10, she courageously protected the bodies of her sons from vultures and other scavengers. She did this from the beginning of the harvest until the drought lifted. Some sources propose that Shimei could have shouted insults at King David on his way to exile in 2 Samuel because of this agreement with the Gibeonites.[1] If that is true, Rizpah spent many sleepless nights fighting vultures to protect her sons' honor.

As Nana Dolce states in her book The Seed of a Woman:

> Her act was daring, whatever its length. This woman,
> accustomed to court luxuries, left every known comfort.
> She shrouded a rock in sackcloth, the sign of mourning,
> and made it her home. Day and night, she suffered the
> putrid stench of seven decaying men. She fought
> plundering birds, by day and by night she stood
> sleeplessly over the bodies of her family so they
> might not suffer the final disgrace of becoming carrion
> for scavenging birds.[2]

In short, Rizpah required David to follow Mosaic Law from Deuteronomy 21:22-23 and bury her sons by protecting her boys' bodies. And God moved on her behalf.

Whose bones did David gather to provide a proper burial with these men's bodies?

Think of those things you've been struggling to sleep through.	Identify scriptures to speak to those situations and prayer.

Access to Guided Prayer

The Scripture That Resonated with Me Today

Thoughts that Come to Mind and Prayers From the Heart

Lesson 3

2 Samuel 23-24

Chapter 23 recounts David's last prophetic words and specifically identified him the son of Jesse, a term Saul attempted to mar in the minds of the Israelite people.

What names has the Lord redeemed on your behalf throughout your life?

It recounts David's last prophecy and then outlines some of David's and his mighty men's great successes. Some stories may stand out as odd, like 2 Samuel 23:16. However, we must remember our cultural standards are completely different.

How could David not drink the water his men had risked their lives to bring him? His men's effort to get him this water was invaluable. It was representative of the fact that God was with them, and that ordinary ground had been transformed. They were yet in a holy place, and David used the water to offer as a drink offering to the One alone who deserved it. The men would have been incredibly honored by this act.

Holy ground was the only place a drink offering would have been acceptable to pour out (Numbers 28:7). Battleground becomes holy ground when you believe the Holy God is helping you. What battleground or hiding place in your own life has been transformed into holy ground?

Despite God's goodness, we continue to see a growing desperation for the Davidic covenant to be fulfilled. Even with protection and a prospering nation all around them, the sraelites continued to exasperate God. We see He allowed the eremy to incite David to conduct a census and count the people (1 Chronicles 21:1). Joab asked him why he would want to do it, but the biographer doesn't share any response, which may do more to help us see David's pride was to blame

more than a response could provide.

There are at least 153 references to pride throughout the Scriptures. What does the Bible say about pride in Proverbs 8:13 and 16:18?

How many men did Joab record during the census?

Recognizing he'd been in a test, David's heart convicted him once the census had been conducted, and he admitted that he'd missed the mark. God is faithful to forgive, but he is equally faithful to discipline us.

What does the Bible say about discipline in Hebrews 12:6?

As a result, the prophet Gad went to the king to ask him if he would rather

1. Three years of famine?
2. Three months of running from his enemies?
3. Three days of plagues?

Out of the three consequences God offered, which did David accept and why in 2 Samuel 24:14?

Which did God send in response (2 Sam 24:15-16)?

David was a leader with integrity, and he requested the anger of the Lord be upon him and his family (a far cry from the finger pointing we conduct today). In response, God sent a message through the prophet Gad. What did God say (2 Sam 24:18)?

We've come full circle in David's reign. David, who conquered Jerusalem by defeating the Jebusites, now had to make an altar to the Lord in the home of a Jebusite. The Lord humbled David's pride by sending the message that all David had, and any victory he had enjoyed, had come from the Lord.

When Araunah asked why David had come, he answered that he was to buy his threshing floor, and Araunah offered to give him anything he might need. However, David insisted. True worship leads you to reflect on the past and admit you have fallen short of God's holy standard as you learn to separate your issues from your identity in Christ. It requires you to take responsibility, reconcile your differences, repent, and rejoice in the Lord's presence.

Psalm 30 is the psalm David wrote to honor the Lord here on Araunah's threshing floor, and he ends it by saying,

> "You turned my wailing into dancing;
>   you removed my sackcloth and clothed me with joy,
>   that my heart may sing your praises and not be silent.
> Lord my God, I will praise you forever."[1]

Selah.

How has the Lord turned your mourning into dancing?

Araunah's threshing floor is the place Abraham first discovered God is Jehovah Jireh, the Lord who provides in Genesis 22, and it later became the location for the temple Solomon built.[2] Mount Moriah is also commonly associated with Golgotha, the place where Jesus was sacrificed on the cross.[3] **Worship alters the atmosphere and establishes an environment of surrender.**

Access to Guided Prayer

The Scripture That Resonated with Me Today

Thoughs that Come to Mind and Prayers From the Heart

Lesson 4

Psalm 2, 3, 16, 22, 110

Athanasius, one of the fourth-century African church fathers whom we celebrate today, once said, "Most of Scripture speaks to us; the Psalms speak for us."[1]

King David was not the only author of the Psalms, but he was the most well-known. Together with the others who wrote the psalms across centuries, he gave some of our deepest pain poetry to help us pray and access God's presence.

You will find seven different genres throughout the book of Psalms ranging from lament to praise. The imprecatory psalms, those written requesting God invoke judgment on one's enemies, are even included. They are some of the most interesting to study. Still, they all point to God's faithfulness as we learn to bring our feelings to God.

What psalm do you find yourself reflecting on most often?

What does this psalm say about God?

What do you find comforting about it?

The books of 1 and 2 Samuel reveal how David's life foreshadowed Jesus' reign and priesthood. However, the Psalms He composed reveal his prophetic nature most.

Most scholars say that David wrote seventy-three Psalms, which does not include Psalm 2. I find it interesting that most of them were of lament. However even more interesting is that many prophesy Jesus' coming.

Psalm 2 is not ascribed to David, but Acts 4:24-26 attributes it to David and because Scripture interprets itself, I have included it here.

Psalm 2

What verses prophesy about the Messiah in Psalm 2?

Compare the language in Psalm 2: 7-9 with

Mathew 1:7-8

Matthew 12:18:

Matthew 17:5:

Hebrews 5:5

Psalm 3

To whom does salvation belong?

Psalm 16

How does Psalm 16:10 foreshadow Jesus' resurrection (reference Acts 2:24-36)?

Psalm 22

What part of Jesus' life does this psalm prophecy about?

Jesus did not speak Hebrew when repeating the words in Psalm 22. He spoke them in Aramaic, but the connection is clear throughout the Psalms that this part of his life foreshadowed the abandonment our King would one day experience from God.

Why was Jesus abandoned by God? (Reference Galatians 3:13-14)

Psalm 110

What words to you see from Psalm 110 repeated in Matthew 22:44?

According to this verse in Matthew, whose Son is the Christ?

Read Acts 2:32-35. What promise did Jesus pour out when He was exalted at God's right hand?

Paul referenced the dual dimension of the Kingdom of God in 1 Corinthians 15:20-28. We understand this concept through the popular phrase George Eldon Ladd coined as "already/not yet." Christ's reign is already here even as we wait for His return (Revelation 22:1-5).

What enemies will become Jesus' footstool (reference 1 Corinthians 15:24-26, Revelation 12:10)?

The one thing I adore about the gift of worship is that our Lord continues to reveal that He is strong enough to redeem any amount of rejection. rebellion, or regret we have suffered. When we surrender shame at hHis feet, Jesus shows us our salvation in Him is secure.

Worship God, in spite of the warfare, because of the warfare, and through the warfare, and you will watch God redeem it all for your good and His glory.

And they conquered him by the blood of the Lamb and by the Word of their testimony, for they loved their lives even unto death (Revelation 12:11 ESV).

Access to Guided Prayer

WORSHIP
GOD AND
WITNESS
HIS
REDEMPTION.

SESSION SIX

Lesson 5

Matthew 1, Luke 1-2, Matthew 27

One of the best things about teaching littles is the delight I see them enjoy when I introduce them to favorite pastimes of my own. Watching this gaming generation attempt to jump rope for the first week is always hilarious, and the sheer joy they exude when they accomplish their goals is the icing on the cake.

Still, they never fail to surprise me. I am always taken aback by how much they love the Where's Waldo puzzle in our classroom because they never tire of it. Even though they know where Waldo is, the amusement never ends, and it captures my heart perfectly about what happens when I encounter Jesus in the Old Testament scriptures every time.

Jesus is our ultimate Prophet, King, and Priest, and a significant portion of scripture throughout 1 and 2 Samuel helps us understand Jesus' role in eternity. The symbolism we find foreshadowing His reign is necessary to understand if we are going to understand how to worship Him more completely.

Jesus As Prophet

Jesus told us He is a prophet in Matthew 13:57. Record the scripture here:

Peter continued to preach about Jesus' role as prophet in Acts as well. Quoting Moses in Deuteronomy 18:15, he encouraged the Jewish members of the early church to remember that all of Scripture speaks of the Anointed One. In fact, he specifically pointed out that all of the prophets from Samuel on prophesied about Jesus and the days of the Church.

I've always found it special that Peter mentioned Samuel because Samuel's life pointed to the Coming Savior and Prophet himself in ways that were never quite mirrored in the other prophets' lives.

From the very beginning, Samuel's mother occupied a unique position in Israel's history. She pushed past a variety of cultural pressures to pray, and, as a result, she procured the attention of the Lord of Heaven's Armies.

But it didn't stop there.

Her prayer not only made an indelible impression on Israelite culture for centuries, but it has continued to impact us throughout the millennia. Mary, the mother of Jesus, even patterned her Magnificat after Hannah's prayer when she sung her response to Elizabeth's blessing.

We notice a progression that parallels Jesus' own process of maturation throughout Samuel's early life.

Fill in the blanks by using the English Standard Version:

1 Samuel 2:21: The boy Samuel grew in the ______________ of the ________________.

1 Samuel 2:26: Now the boy Samuel continued to grow in ______________ and in ______________ with the __________ and also with ______________.

1 Samuel 3:19: And Samuel ______________ and the Lord was with him, and let ____________ of his ______________ fall to the __________________.

Compare these verses with those written about Jesus in Luke.

Luke 2:40: And the ________________ grew and became ____________, filled with ______________. And the ____________ of ______________ was upon him.

Luke 2:52: And ______________ increased in ______________ and in ________________ and in ______________ with ________________ and ____________________.

Samuel proved to be a kind and gracious prophet, and the Lord never allowed his words to fall to the ground. Furthermore, He revealed himself to Samuel by the word of the Lord, paving the way for the Word of the Lord, Jesus Christ.

Jesus As King

As we have learned, Hannah was not only a powerful prayer warrior, but a prophet, as well. In 1 Samuel 2, Hannah first prophesied of a king decades before one would ever ever ascend the throne and centuries before Jesus would be revealed in 1 Samuel 2:10.

1 Samuel 2:10 reads: "The adversaries of the Lord shall be broken to pieces; against them he will thunder in heaven. The Lord will judge the ends of the earth; he will give strength to his king and exalt the horn of his anointed" (ESV).

Revelation 19:11-16 reiterates this. Record the names of Jesus that you find in Revelation 19:11-16 below:

Jesus's role as king is exemplified throughout David's life, as well. Most of David's life pointed to a just king. However, the characteristics that fail to compare instead confess a need for the True King, apart from whom all will fall.

Once David professed a desire to build the Lord a house, the Lord responded He, Himself, would lead one of David's sons to build a house for Him. As Vina Mogg so poignantly writes, "The framework of two timbers in the shape of a cross established the house of God on this earth."

God, in His omniscience (all-knowing), continued to say He would discipline Jesus (David's son) with the rod of men, with the stripes of the sons of men and that through His correction, David's throne would be established forever.

Jesus, the Word that Became Flesh, continued to retain all power in His hands, even while on earth. Nevertheless, He chose to restrain that power so that we might be restored to relationship with the Father.

Which son of David is named in Matthew 1:7?

Which son of David is named in Luke 3:31)?

Note, some scholars believe that Luke actually accounts for Mary's lineage, but names Joseph in her place because biographers didn't account for women.[1]

When the Roman soldiers who had come to arrest Him asked if Jesus was the Jesus of Nazareth, His answer caused them to fall back in submission to His strength (John 18:6). Yet, He told the disciples that He could have asked His Father for twelve legions of angels, and yet would instead fulfill the Scriptures (Matthew 27:53-54)

Instead, He decided to restrain Himself and endure the Cross, despising the shame, for the joy set before Him. Today His name, Yahweh, denoting His exalted status and relationship with the Father, is the name above every name. His name is known in Hebrew as Yeshua, Iēsous in Greek, and Jesus in English, and at the mention of it, every knee will bow in heaven and on earth and under the earth, and every tongue will confess that Jesus Christ is Lord, to the glory of the Father (Philippians 2:9-11).

Jesus As Priest

David was the only king who served as king and priest before the Lord.

Time and time again, David requested his ephod be brought to him so he could inquire of the Lord. The ephod was a garment high priests wore over their shoulders before they prayed to the Lord for direction, and the only time David refrained from having it brought was when He asked for the ark.

When David retrieved the ark from Obed-Edom's house, he wore that ephod prophetically, sacrificed to the Lord, and danced before Him, too.

When he walked in the wilderness on his way into exile, he sacrificed before the Lord and inquired of the ark of the Lord. The Scriptures continue to remind us how David served before the Lord openly in the tent, and David's God is distinguished by the intimate relationship He shared with David in ways that were never again replicated in the Old Testament (Amos 9:11 and Acts 15:16-17). Whether that signifies that the tent David worshiped in was as different in the natural as it was the spiritual, as some believe, is yet to be understood. What remains certain, however, is that David was unlike any other priest before him, and yet, he still paled in comparison to our Priest.

Our High Priest was tested in every way and yet was still without sin.

What is the difference that Hebrews 4:14-16 describes about our High Priest in Jesus in comparison to every other priest in Scripture?

In Matthew 27:50-51, we read that Jesus yielded His spirit and the curtain in the temple was torn in two, from top to bottom. What does this mean for us? (Hebrews 4:16)

Jesus is known as a priest forever after the order of Melchizedek, and He was given this status once He humbled Himself. How can we honor Him today? In what areas do you feel the Lord humbling you? How could that work together for your good?

Cultivate a
reputation
for worship.

The Scripture That Resonated with Me Today

Thoughs that Come to Mind and Prayers From the Heart

APPENDIX A

Session One, Lesson One

A Conversation on Mental Health
with Kobe Campbell

Session One, Lesson Two

A Conversation on Church Hurt
with Pricelis Perreaux-Dominguez

Session Two, Lesson One

A Conversation on Harmful Theology
with Jennifer Lucy Tyler

Session One, Lesson Two

A Conversation on Distraction
with Katie Westenberg

A P P E N D I X   A

Session Three, Lesson Five

A Conversation on Pressure
with Naila Tee

Session Two, Lesson One

A Conversation on Waiting
with Oghosa Iyamu

Session Two, Lesson Two

A Conversation on Sacrifice
with Brenna Blain

Session Two, Lesson Two

A Friend Like Jonathan
a Sermon by Liv Dooley

Session Two, Lesson Two

A Conversation on Identity
with Tasha Jun

APPENDIX A

Session Two, Lesson Two

A Conversation on Idolaty
with Elizabeth Woodson

Session Three, Lesson Five

A Conversation on Identity
with Dr. Heather Thompson Day

Session Four, Lesson Two

A Conversation on Father Wounds
with Kia Stephens

Session Four, Lesson Three

A Conversation on Love & Holiness
with Phylicia Masonheimer

Session Four, Lesson Three

A Conversation on Calling
with Jo Saxton

APPENDIX A

Session Four, Lesson Four

A Conversation on Worship
with Kanita Rutley

Session Four, Lesson Five

A Conversation on Disability
with Jennifer Ji-Hye Ko

Session Five, Lesson Three

A Conversation on Sexual Abuse
with Mary Demuth

Session Five, Lesson Three

A Conversation on Grief
with Natasha Smith

Session Five, Lesson Four

A Conversation on Children Who Rebel
with Pamela Henkleman

APPENDIX A

Session Five, Lesson Five

A Conversation on the Wilderness
with Faith Eury Cho

Session Five, Lesson Five

The Power of Prayer
a Sermon by Liv Dooley

Session Six, Lesson Three

A Conversation on Unfamiliar Women
in the Bible with Nana Dolce

Session Six, Lesson Four

A Conversation on Jesus and the Psalms
with Barb Roose

ENDNOTES

Introduction

1. <u>Selah</u>. (2016). In J. D. Barry, D. Bomar, D. R. Brown, R. Klippenstein, D. Mangum, C. Sinclair Wolcott, L. Wentz, E. Ritzema, & W. Widder (Eds.), The Lexham Bible Dictionary. Lexham Press.
2. Lyon, Ashley. "What Does Selah Mean?" Logos.Com, Logos , Jan. 2023, https://www.logos.com/grow/bsm-what-does-selah-mean/.
3. Noyes, Penny. "What Does Selah Mean in the Bible?" Christianity.Com, Christianity.com, 11 Apr. 2022, https://www.christianity.com/wiki/christian-terms/what-does-selah-mean-in-the-bible.html.
4. Kranz, Jeffrey. "Who Wrote the Psalms? Hint: Not Just David." OverviewBible, 12 Oct. 2018, https://overviewbible.com/who-wrote-psalms-besides-david/.
5. Anderson, J. E. (2016). <u>Samuel, First and Second Books of</u>. In J. D. Barry, D. Bomar, D. R. Brown, R. Klippenstein, D. Mangum, C. Sinclair Wolcott, L. Wentz, E. Ritzema, & W. Widder (Eds.), The Lexham Bible Dictionary. Lexham Press.
6. Evans, Tony, and Bibles Holman. The Tony Evans Bible Commentary. B&H Publishing Group, 2019, p. 292.

Session One, Lesson One

1. "Your Brain at Work: The Reticular Activating System (RAS) and Your Goals & Behaviour." Change Management & Organisational Development: The Latest Neuroscience to Boost Your Business, https://lifexchangesolutions.com/reticular-activating-system/. Accessed 13 June 2023.
2. "1 Samuel 2 (KJV) - Moreover His Mother Made Him." Blue Letter Bible, https://www.blueletterbible.org/kjv/1sa/2/19/t_conc_238019. Accessed 13 June 2023.
3. "The Best Kept Secret With Liv Dooley: Helping Others Heal From Church Hurt with Pricelis Perreaux-Dominguez on Apple Podcasts." Apple Podcasts, 28 Nov. 2022,https://podcasts.apple.com/us/podcast/helping-others-heal-from-church-hurt-with-pricelis/id1551475351?i=1000587724839.

Session One, Lesson Three

1. "Comparison Definition & Meaning - Merriam-Webster." Merriam-Webster: America's Most Trusted

Session One, Lesson Three (cont'd)

Dictionary, https://www.merriamwebster.com/dictionary/comparison. Accessed 14 June 2023.
2. Beaty, Katelyn. Celebrities for Jesus. Brazos Press, 2022, p. 14.

Session One, Lesson Four

1. Masonheimer, Phylicia. Every Woman a Theologian. Thomas Nelson, 2023, p. 32.

Session 2, Lesson One

1. Davis, Tchiki. "Regret: What Is It and How to Deal With It - The Berkeley Well-Being Institute." The Berkeley Well-Being Institute, https://www.berkeleywellbeing.com/regret.html. Accessed 14 June 2023.
2. Anyabwile, Thabiti. "Filtered Listening, 5: Conviction and Condemnation." The Gospel Coalition, https://www.facebook.com/thegospelcoalition/, 22 Feb. 2010, https://www.thegospelcoalition.org/blogs/thabiti-anyabwile/filtered-listening-5-conviction-and-condemnation/.

Session Two, Lesson Two

1. "Enduring Word Bible Commentary 1 Samuel Chapter 15." Enduring Word, https://www.facebook.com/HisWordEndures/, 27 Dec. 2015, https://enduringword.com/bible-commentary/1-samuel-15/.

Session Two, Lesson Three

1. Richards, E. Randolph, and Brandon J. O'Brien. Misreading Scripture with Western Eyes. InterVarsity Press, 2012, p. 12.
2. Deffinbaugh, Bob. "4. Waiting on the Lord (2 Samuel 2:1-5:5) | Bible.Org." Bible.Org | Where the World Comes to Study the Bible, 1 June 2004, https://bible.org/seriespage/4-waiting-lord-2-samuel-21-55.
3. Masonheimer, Phylicia. Every Woman a Theologian. Thomas Nelson, 2023, p. 117.
4. Barry, J. D., Mangum, D., Brown, D. R., Heiser, M. S., Custis, M., Ritzema, E., Whitehead, M. M., Grigoni, M.

ENDNOTES

Session Two, Lesson Three (cont'd)

R., & Bomar, D. (2012, 2016). <u>Faithlife Study Bible</u> (1 Sa 16:18). Lexham Press.
2. Richards, E. Randolph, and Richard James. Misreading Scripture with Individualist Eyes. InterVarsity Press, 2020, p. 44.

Session Two, Lesson Four

1. Richards, E. Randolph, and Richard James. Misreading Scripture with Individualist Eyes. InterVarsity Press, 2020, p. 15.
2. Raucher, Michal. "Rachel Leans In - Jewish Theological Seminary." Jewish Theological Seminary, https://www.facebook.com/JewishTheologicalSeminary/, 5 Nov. 2013, https://www.jtsa.edu/torah/rachel-leans-in/.
3. Roberts, Mark. "When Trusting God Isn't Good Enough - De Pree Center." Fuller De Pree Center, 1 Dec. 2015, https://depree.org/when-trusting-god-isnt-good-enough/.
4. "Enduring Word Bible Commentary 1 Samuel Chapter 19." Enduring Word, Enduring Word Bible Commentary, 27 Dec. 2015, https://enduringword.com/bible-commentary/1-samuel-19/.

Session Two, Lesson Five
1. Gay, Jr., Jerome. Church Hurt: Holding the Church Accountable and Helping Hurt People Heal . Renown Publishing, 2023, p. 6.

Session Three, Lesson One
1. "En Gedi (BiblePlaces.Com)." BiblePlaces.Com, https://www.bibleplaces.com/engedi/. Accessed 15 June 2023.
2. Richards, E. Randolph, and Richard James. Misreading Scripture with Individualist Eyes. InterVarsity Press, 2020, p. 24.
3. Terkeurst, Lysa. "3 S's of Connectivity, Part 2." Compeltraining.Com, Compel Training, https://compeltraining.com/lesson/3-ss-of-connectivity-part-2-2-2/. Accessed 15 June 2023.

Session Three, Lesson Two
1. Bricker, Vivian. "What Should Christians Know about Psychics?" Christianity.Com, Christianity.com, 14 June 2022, https://www.christianity.com/wiki/cults-and-other-religions/what-should-christians-know-about-psychics.html.
2. "Leviticus 19 (KJV) - Regard Not Them That Have." Blue Letter Bible, https://www.blueletterbible.org/kjv/lev/19/31/t_conc_109031. Accessed 15 June 2023.
3. Masonheimer, Phylicia. Every Woman a Theologian. Thomas Nelson, 2023, p. 115.
4. "Americans Continue to Redefine - and Reject - God." American Worldview Inventory 2020 - At a Glance, Cultural Reseach Center, 21 Apr. 2020, https://www.arizonachristian.edu/wp-content/uploads/2020/04/CRC-AWVI-2020-Release-03_Perceptions-of-God.pdf.

Session Three, Lesson Four
1. "Counteractive Definition & Meaning - Merriam-Webster." Merriam-Webster: America's Most Trusted Dictionary, https://www.merriam-webster.com/dictionary/counteractive. Accessed 15 June 2023.

Session Three, Lesson Five
1. "H2388 - Ḥāzaq - Strong's Hebrew Lexicon (Kjv)." Blue Letter Bible, https://www.blueletterbible.org/lexicon/h2388/kjv/wlc/0-1/. Accessed 15 June 2023.

Session Four, Lesson Two
1. Richards, E. Randolph, and Richard James. Misreading Scripture with Individualist Eyes. InterVarsity Press, 2020, p. 47.
2. Richards, E. Randolph, and Richard James. Misreading Scripture with Individualist Eyes. InterVarsity Press, 2020, p. 48.
3. Stephens, Kia. Overcoming Father Wounds. Baker Books, 2023, p. 124.

Session Four, Lesson Three

1. "The Consecration of the Coronation Oil." Royal.Uk, The Royal Household, 2023, https://www.royal.uk/news-and-activity/2023-03-03/the-consecration-of-the-coronation-oil.

ENDNOTES

Session Four, Lesson Three (cont'd)

2. Davies, Madeleine. "UK Coronation Remains Religious, Even If the Country Isn't | Christianity Today." ChristianityToday.Com, Christianity Today, 2 May 2023, https://www.christianitytoday.com/ct/2023/may-web-only/uk-king-charles-coronation-church-of-england-religious-mona.html.

3. The Holy Bible: English Standard Version (1 Sam 7:2). (2016). Crossway Bibles.

4. The Holy Bible: English Standard Version (Ac 13:21). (2016). Crossway Bibles.

5. Barry, J. D., Mangum, D., Brown, D. R., Heiser, M. S., Custis, M., Ritzema, E., Whitehead, M. M., Grigoni, M. R., & Bomar, D. (2012, 2016). Faithlife Study Bible (2 Sa 6:2). Lexham Press.

6. Masonheimer, Phylicia. Every Woman a Theologian. Thomas Nelson, 2023, p. 31.

7. Dooley, Liv, host. "Leading Beyond Brokenness, Regret, and Jealousy with Jo Saxton." *The Best Kept Secret with Liv Dooley*, episode75, Red Circle, 27. Mar 2023, livdooley.com/josaxton

8. Fritch, David. Enthroned. Burning Ones, 2017, p. 23.

9. Lisitsa, Ellie. "The Four Horsemen: Criticism, Contempt, Defensiveness, & Stonewalling." The Gottman Institute, The Gottman Institute, 24 Apr. 2013, https://www.gottman.com/blog/the-four-horsemen-recognizing-criticism-contempt-defensiveness-and-stonewalling/.

Session Four, Lesson Five

1. Barry, J. D., Mangum, D., Brown, D. R., Heiser, M. S., Custis, M., Ritzema, E., Whitehead, M. M., Grigoni, M. R., & Bomar, D. (2012, 2016). Faithlife Study Bible (2 Sa 9:7). Lexham Press.

2. Georges, Jayson, and Mark D. Baker. Ministering in Honor-Shame Cultures. InterVarsity Press, 2016, p. 30.

Session Five, Lesson Two

1. Richards, E. Randolph, and Brandon J. O'Brien. Misreading Scripture with Western Eyes. InterVarsity Press, 2012, p. 45.

2. The Holy Bible: English Standard Version (2 Sa 23:39). (2016). Crossway Bibles.

3. Barry, J. D., Mangum, D., Brown, D. R., Heiser, M. S., Custis, M., Ritzema, E., Whitehead, M. M., Grigoni, M. R., & Bomar, D. (2012, 2016). Faithlife Study Bible (2 Sa 11:8). Lexham Press.

Session Five, Lesson Two (cont'd)

5. Richards, E. Randolph, and Brandon J. O'Brien. Misreading Scripture with Western Eyes. InterVarsity Press, 2012, p. 45.

Session Five, Lesson Three

1. The Bible Says. "Deuteronomy 22:28-29 Meaning | TheBibleSays.Com." TheBibleSays.Com, https://thebiblesays.com/commentary, 13 July 2022, https://thebiblesays.com/commentary/deut/deut-22/deuteronomy-2228-29/.

2. Barry, J. D., Mangum, D., Brown, D. R., Heiser, M. S., Custis, M., Ritzema, E., Whitehead, M. M., Grigoni, M. R., & Bomar, D. (2012, 2016). Faithlife Study Bible (2 Sa 13:24). Lexham Press.

Session Five, Lesson Four

1. Kohn, Rebbetzin Leah. "The Woman of Tekoa: A Proper Use of Personal Talent • Torah.Org." Torah.Org, https://torah.org/, 24 June 2020, https://torah.org/learning/women-class66/.

2. Camp, Claudia V.. "Wise Woman of Tekoa: Bible." Shalvi/Hyman Encyclopedia of Jewish Women. 31 December 1999. Jewish Women's Archive. (Viewed on June 18, 2023) <https://jwa.org/encyclopedia/article/wise-woman-of-tekoa-bible>.

3. https://bibleatlas.org/tekoa.htm

4. Camp, Claudia V.. "Wise Woman of Tekoa: Bible." Shalvi/Hyman Encyclopedia of Jewish Women. 31 December 1999. Jewish Women's Archive. (Viewed on June 18, 2023) <https://jwa.org/encyclopedia/article/wise-woman-of-tekoa-bible>.

5. Kohn, Rebbetzin Leah. "The Woman of Tekoa: A Proper Use of Personal Talent • Torah.Org." Torah.Org, https://torah.org/, 24 June 2020, https://torah.org/learning/women-class66/.

6. Kohn, Rebbetzin Leah. "The Woman of Tekoa: A Proper Use of Personal Talent • Torah.Org." Torah.Org, https://torah.org/, 24 June 2020, https://torah.org/learning/women-class66/.

Session Five, Lesson Five

1. Endor speak of necromancy and divination. The witch of Endor and Zadok the priest, were different, and the fruit they bore demonstrates that. Prophecy leads us to become more intimate with

ENDNOTES

Session Five, Lesson Five (cont'd)

2. "Trending Faith: Is It Okay to Visit a Psychic for Fun?
   GCU Blogs." GCU, 23 Feb. 2016,
   https://www.gcu.edu/blog/theology-
   ministry/trending-faith-it-okay-visit-psychic-fun.

Session Six, Lesson Two
1. Barry, J. D., Mangum, D., Brown, D. R., Heiser, M. S.,
   Custis, M., Ritzema, E., Whitehead, M. M., Grigoni, M.
   R., & Bomar, D. (2012, 2016). Faithlife Study Bible (2
   Sa 16:7). Lexham Press.
2. Dolce, Nana. The Seed of the Woman. Evangelical
   Press, 2022, p. 137.

Session Six, Lesson Three

1. "Probable Timeline of When Each Psalm Was Written
   - Study Resources." Blue Letter Bible,
   https://www.blueletterbible.org/study/parallel/par
   al18.cfm. Accessed 18 June 2023.
2. Barry, J. D., Mangum, D., Brown, D. R., Heiser, M. S.,
   Custis, M., Ritzema, E., Whitehead, M. M., Grigoni, M.
   R., & Bomar, D. (2012, 2016). Faithlife Study Bible
   (Ge 22:2). Lexham Press.
3. Cooper, Melinda Eye. "3 Reasons Mount Moriah
   Matters to Us Today - Bible Study." Crosswalk.Com,
   Crosswalk.com, 3 Nov. 2021,
   https://www.crosswalk.com/faith/bible-
   study/reasons-the-events-at-mount-moriah-are-
   important-to-us-today.html.

Session Six, Lesson Four

1. "The Psalms - Adult Christian Formation." Adult
   Christian Formation, Episcopal Diocese of West
   Texas, 22 Apr. 2020, https://christianformation-
   dwtx.org/the-psalms/.

Session Six, Lesson Five
1. "Is Mary's Lineage in One of the Gospels? |
   Bible.Org." Bible.Org | Where the World Comes to
   Study the Bible, 1 Jan. 2001,
   https://bible.org/question/mary%E2%80%99s-
   lineage-one-gospels.

ACKNOWLEDGEMENTS

The Church girl in me needs to first give honor and glory to my Heavenly Father, who is the head of my life and has matured me in every way during this study. My God, You and You alone know how many tears I cried during the writing and the release of this study. I cannot thank You enough for impressing this work upon my heart.

 I am so very bad at acknowledgments, so if I forget your name, please charge it to my head and not my heart. Now, enough of the Christianese. LOL.

I'd like to thank my husband, Frantavious Dooley. I thank God for how you have always encouraged me to believe that I could write this study. I bless God for your support, and I thank You for pausing to weather the storms we've faced together time and time again. Session three brought me to tears when I wrote about how you have helped me experience the renewal worship brings, and I pray you experience it every day of your life.

To my mom, who has sat through countless sermons as I've shared the content of this study over the past five years. I am amazed by how you still show excitement after having heard the same content year after year. Dad, I appreciate how often you let me steal Mom away for those women's events. I cannot thank you for the unconditional love you share and the confidence you instill within me to do everything I feel called by God to do.

Mama Jennifer, thank you for celebrating various milestones with me, praying for me, and continuing to encourage my heart through this process.

Dr. Quantrilla Ard, how I love you, sister! Thank you for laboring over this project with me in the first few years of its inception. It is a Bible study because of your leadership, and I cannot thank you enough for all of the words you spoke over my writing.

To my sister-mama-auntie-friends-and-them in the focus group, I cannot thank You enough for how you helped me offer a concise study to lead others through the books of First and Second Samuel. Mama Barb, Ms. Christine, Desirée, Tonya, and Mom, I adore your lives, and I am better in every way because you are in my life.

Jacque, Arnette, Tina, and Ms. Maryann, I bless God for moving you to give to this goal. There were days I felt like I was scrimping pennies, and even though I know that was far from the case, your generosity helped remind me that I am not alone.

I have come a long way from the first book I released in 2014. Back then, the thought of having to talk about my writing was intimidating in every way. Over the years, though, I have learned how to have fun. Each and every woman who participated in the panels I had the opportunity to gather together around this message made this endeavor so much more fun. Prepping for our time together helped me continue working until the very end, and I bless God for your belief in this work well before you ever laid eyes on it.

Dr. Parson, it was an absolute honor to interview you about the role our mental health plays in our Christian journey. You have had a considerable influence on my life, and I cannot thank you enough for the days you delayed your own vacation to ensure that I could drive home without harming myself all those years ago. I can never pay you back, but it is my prayer I can one day pay it forward.

To the women who have prayed with me at any point in time throughout the process of this book. I cannot say that it would be here in our hands today had it not been your choice to answer the Holy Spirit's unction: Shalisha, Zatoyic, Tricia, December, Mama Heidi, Sharonda, Sheila, Malika, Sylvia, Jackie, Neyda, Arnette, Jocque, Tina, Veronica, Zareuh, Cecori, Ms. Connie, Jennifer, Michanda, Ty, Phylicia, Kanita, Pricelis, Brenna, Kristen, my NCC prayer pod, and the prayer team for Entrusted Women. Please know I am in your corner, and I am cheering you on!

Abbey, girl. I cannot thank you enough for the content you labored over to help me provide a concise and, prayerfully helpful, guide to the readers, here. You are such a blessing, and there were so many times where I was blessed by your commentary throughout the editing process of this book.

Janelle, I prayed God would send along someone He'd blessed to capture the vision for the cover and then he sent you. Thank you for all you did to help me feel confident about presenting this book to the world.

Lastly, I want to thank every church that has welcomed me and every small group that has included Selah in their curriculum. I am overwhelmed by your love. May I say a special thank you to Jeremy and Lindsey Bosma? Thank you for inviting me to speak at your church for the sermon series you hosted on 1 and 2 Samuel during the release of *Selah*. I cannot thank God enough for your beautiful church community and the gift of your friendship.

The Scripture That Resonated with Me Today

Thoughs that Come to Mind and Prayers From the Heart

The Scripture That Resonated with Me Today

Thoughs that Come to Mind and Prayers From the Heart

The Scripture That Resonated with Me Today

Thoughs that Come to Mind and Prayers From the Heart

The Scripture That Resonated with Me Today

Thoughs that Come to Mind and Prayers From the Heart